Letts

GCSE

VISUAL
REVISION
GUIDE

SUCCESS

QUESTIONS & ANSWERS

& ANSWERS

GEOGRAPHY

Author
Adam Arnell

CONTENTS

HOMEWORK DIARY

TOPIC	SCORE
Tectonic activity	/27
Earthquakes	/26
Volcanoes	/28
Rocks	/25
Landforms	/28
River processes	/28
River landforms	/30
Flooding	/25
Coastal processes	/29
Coastal landforms	/30
Coastal management	/30
Glaciation	/29
Glacial landforms	/30
Weather	/30
Climate	/30
Weather and people	/33
Population	/29
Changing populations	/25
Migration	/30
Settlement	/30
Settlement in MEDCs	/27
Settlement in LEDCs	/27
Agriculture	/30
Agricultural change	/30
Industry	/27
Industry in MEDCs	/30
Industry in LEDCs	/30
Tourism	/30
Tourism case studies	/29
Resources	/30
Energy	/30
Development	/30
Trade and aid	/30
Ecosystems	/30
Global environments	/30
Global warming	/30
Acid rain	/30
Use and abuse of the environment – water	/28
Use and abuse of the environment – land	/30
Map skills	/30

EXAM HINTS

- Read the information on the <u>front page of the exam paper</u>. This will tell you <u>how many</u> questions you should answer. If you have a <u>choice</u> of questions, make absolutely sure that you <u>answer questions on the topics you have studied</u>.

- Read through <u>all the questions</u> that you are going to answer, then begin with the one you <u>know best</u>.

- Highlight the <u>command</u> words and make sure you <u>answer the question</u>. For example, does it say '<u>describe</u>' or '<u>explain</u>'? Does it ask for <u>examples</u>?

- Before the exam find out <u>how many marks</u> are available and <u>how long</u> the exam will take. Divide the number of minutes by the number of marks to work out the <u>time available for each mark</u>. You should find you have about <u>1 minute per mark</u>.

- Use the number of marks available for each question to <u>guide you</u> on how many <u>points</u> you need to make and <u>how much to write</u>.

- <u>Stick to your schedule</u> during the exam. The <u>first marks</u> are the easiest to gain, so <u>don't waste time</u> trying to pick up extra marks when you should be <u>moving on</u> to the next question.

- Learn the <u>technical geographical words</u>, and then <u>use them</u> in the exam. You will gain marks for the <u>quality of your language</u>.

- Learn your <u>case studies</u> well, and be prepared to give a <u>good level of detail</u>.

- Don't be afraid to use case studies that you did not study in class. For example, if you have seen a case study of a flood on television, and can remember the details, <u>use it in your exam</u>.

- Make sure you can carry out all the <u>basic geographical skills</u>, such as four-figure and six-figure grid references.

- <u>Plan</u> your answers to the questions which require <u>extended writing</u> – this will ensure that you include all the <u>important points</u> you wish to make.

- Try to show that you see the '<u>bigger picture</u>'. This means looking at geographical ideas at different scales from <u>local</u> to <u>global</u>. For example, the global impact of global warming may be a rise in sea level, whereas a local impact may be more mosquitoes.

- Show how geographical processes are <u>linked together</u>, especially <u>human</u> and <u>physical</u> processes. For example, an increase in the number of refugees will have a negative impact on the natural environment as demand for food, water and fuel increases.

- Remember that <u>impacts</u> or <u>effects</u> of geographical processes may be <u>physical</u> or <u>human</u>, and that these impacts can be <u>positive</u> or <u>negative</u>.

- Diagrams must be <u>well annotated</u>. Annotations are <u>detailed comments</u>, which may be <u>descriptive</u> or <u>explanatory</u>.

TECTONIC ACTIVITY

A

Choose just one answer, a, b, c or d.

1 The temperature of the Earth's core is
(a) 1,200°C
(b) 5,000°C
(c) 5,500°C
(d) 8,500°C   (1 mark)

2 An ocean trench is formed at a
(a) Constructive boundary
(b) Destructive boundary
(c) Collision boundary
(d) Conservative boundary   (1 mark)

3 The Earth's surface is made up of how many tectonic plates?
(a) 1   (c) 7
(b) 12   (d) 19   (1 mark)

4 Tectonic plates slide past each other at a
(a) Constructive boundary
(b) Destructive boundary
(c) Collision boundary
(d) Conservative boundary   (1 mark)

5 Volcanoes are distributed across the Earth's surface
(a) In a randomly distributed pattern
(b) In an evenly distributed pattern
(c) In long narrow bands
(d) Under the oceans   (1 mark)

Score   /5

B

Answer all parts of all questions.

1 Cross out the incorrect words in the sentences below.

(a) A constructive plate boundary is where two plates are ~~diverging~~/converging.

(b) At destructive plate boundaries, oceanic/~~continental~~ crust is melted and destroyed.

(c) Fold mountains are formed at ~~conservative~~/collision plate boundaries.

(d) At conservative plate boundaries, the most dangerous hazard is earthquakes/~~volcanoes~~.

(e) A collision boundary occurs where two ~~oceanic~~/continental plates are converging.

(f) Mid-ocean ridges are found at ~~destructive~~/constructive plate boundaries.   (6 marks)

2 Give a located example of each of the following types of plate boundary.

(a) Constructive   Mid Atlantic Ridge

(b) Destructive   Japan

(c) Collision   India

(d) Conservative   San Andreas Fault   (4 marks)

Score   /10

These are GCSE-style questions. Answer all parts of the questions.

1 Study the map below, which shows the location of major tectonic plates, earthquake zones and volcanic areas.

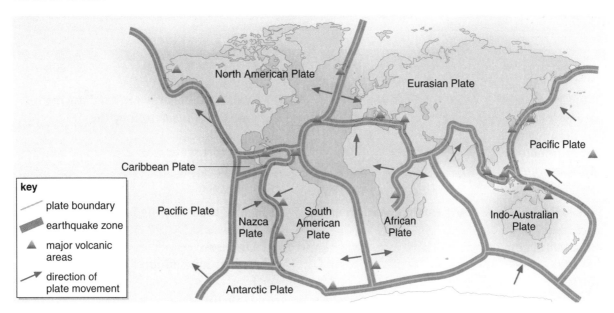

(a) What evidence is there that tectonic plates are able to move across the Earth's surface?

There is evidence from volcanoes and earthquakes

(2 marks)

(b) Suggest how tectonic plates are able to move. You may use a diagram to help you.

The Earth's core is extremely hot. This causes convection currents in the mantle. This current moves the tectonic plates

(4 marks)

(c) Describe and explain the relationship between the location of volcanoes and earthquakes shown in the map.

Earthquakes are located near plate boundaries. Volcanoes only located in some areas. There is not pattern for this. Volcanoes are also located on or near a plate boundary

(6 marks)

Score   /12

How well did you do?

1–7 correct   Try again
8–14 correct   Getting there
15–20 correct   Good work
21–27 correct   Excellent!

TOTAL SCORE   /27

**For more on this topic
see pages 4–5 of your Success Guide**

EARTHQUAKES

A

Choose just one answer, a, b, c or d.

1 What instrument is used to record the strength of an earthquake?
(a) Seismograph
(b) Barometer
(c) Seismometer ⊙
(d) Tilt meter   (1 mark)

2 Approximately how many earthquakes occur each year?
(a) 2,000
(b) 6,000 ⊙
(c) 10,000 ⊙
(d) 60,000   (1 mark)

3 The place underground where an earthquake starts is called the
(a) Epicentre   (b) Fault line
(c) Seismic wave   (d) Focus ⊙   (1 mark)

4 The amount of energy released during an earthquake is measured by the
(a) Mercalli scale
(b) Beaufort scale
(c) Richter scale ⊙
(d) Fujita scale   (1 mark)

5 Which of the following is a primary effect of an earthquake?
(a) Disease
(b) Collapsing buildings ⊙
(c) Fire
(d) Tsunami   (1 mark)

Score /5

B

Answer all parts of all questions.

1 Study the diagrams below.

Seismometer

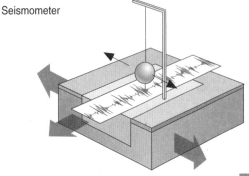

Seismograph

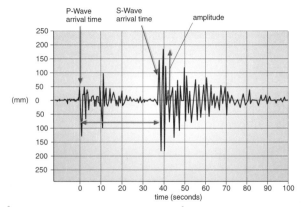

(a) Describe how a seismometer works. _It detects the amplitude of P and S waves and records their arrival times_ (3 marks)

(b) What is a seismic wave? _Shock wave_ (1 mark)

(c) Which type of seismic wave travels most quickly? _P - Wave_ (1 mark)

(d) Which type of seismic wave is most powerful? _S - Wave_ (1 mark)

(e) What is the time interval between the P-waves and the S-waves shown on the seismograph?
40 seconds (1 mark)

Score /7

8

C **These are GCSE-style questions. Answer all parts of the questions.**

1 Study the map below, which shows details of the earthquake that struck Turkey in 1999.

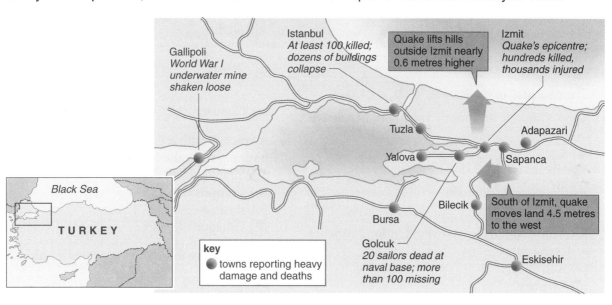

Gallipoli
World War I underwater mine shaken loose

Istanbul
At least 100 killed; dozens of buildings collapse

Quake lifts hills outside Izmit nearly 0.6 metres higher

Izmit
Quake's epicentre; hundreds killed, thousands injured

Tuzla

Adapazari

Yalova

Sapanca

Black Sea

TURKEY

Bilecik

South of Izmit, quake moves land 4.5 metres to the west

Bursa

Golcuk
20 sailors dead at naval base; more than 100 missing

Eskisehir

key
● towns reporting heavy damage and deaths

(a) Describe the impact of the earthquake on:

(i) the natural environment ...Underwater mine shaken loose, hills outside Izmit lifted 0.6 high...

(2 marks)

(ii) people ...Izmit: 100's killed 1000's injured   Istanbul: 100's killed...

(2 marks)

(b) Explain why the earthquake in Turkey may have occurred.

...Pressure built up at plate boundary causing plate to jerk. Thus releasing shock waves called seismic waves...

(4 marks)

(c) Suggest how the Turkish people might prepare for future earthquakes.

...Emergency plans and earthquake drill. Stronger buildings. Early warning systems like a siren etc. However Turkey has limited funding so all this would be difficult to achieve...

(6 marks)

Score   /14

How well did you do?
0–7 correct   Try again
8–13 correct   Getting there
14–20 correct   Good work
21–26 correct   Excellent!

TOTAL SCORE   /26

For more on this topic see pages 6–7 of your Success Guide

VOLCANOES

A

Choose just one answer, a, b, c or d.

1 Approximately how many volcanoes are active worldwide?
(a) 8
(b) 80
(c) 800
(d) 8,000 (1 mark)

2 A volcano which has not erupted for 200 years is described as
(a) Active
(b) Dormant
(c) Extinct
(d) Expired (1 mark)

3 Composite volcanoes are found on which type of plate boundary?
(a) Constructive
(b) Destructive
(c) Collision
(d) Conservative (1 mark)

4 A volcano which does not occur on a plate boundary is called a
(a) Shield volcano
(b) Composite volcano
(c) Basic volcano
(d) Hotspot volcano (1 mark)

5 Which of the following describes a shield volcano?
(a) Wide base with gently sloping sides
(b) Narrow base with gently sloping sides
(c) Wide base with steep sides
(d) Narrow base with steep sides (1 mark)

Score /5

B

Answer all parts of all questions.

1 Match the following volcano types to the correct example.

Shield — Mauna Loa, Hawaii
Composite — Mt St Helens, USA
Hotspot — Mt Etna, Italy

(3 marks)

2 Match the following descriptions of volcanic eruptions with the key words.

(a) A river of molten rock up to 1,200°C.

Lava flow

(b) A cloud of red-hot gas and ash moving at 200 km/hour.

Pyroclastic flow

(c) A mixture of volcanic ash and rainwater.

Mud flow

(d) Pulverised rock and lava falling back to Earth.

Ash fall (4 marks)

pyroclastic flow • ash fall • mud flow • lava flow

Score /7

These are GCSE-style questions. Answer all parts of the questions.

1 Study the photograph, which shows the impact of the volcanic eruption in Montserrat in 1995. Montserrat is an island in the Caribbean.

(a) Describe the impacts of the eruption shown by the photograph.

Destroys environment: Dusty ash. Buildings damaged (2 marks)

(b) Suggest why Montserrat has experienced a number of explosive volcanic eruptions in recent years.

Montserrat is located on a destructive plate boundary. South American is being forced below the Caribbean plate. Causes (4 marks)
magma to rise
through cracks
mantle

(c) Describe the long-term effects of a volcanic eruption you have studied.

....

....

....

.... (4 marks)

(d) Explain how scientists are able to predict volcanic eruptions with increasing accuracy.

....

....

....

....

.... (6 marks)

Score   /16

How well did you do?

0–7 correct   Try again
8–14 correct   Getting there
15–21 correct   Good work
22–28 correct   Excellent!

TOTAL SCORE   /28

**For more on this topic
see pages 8–9 of your Success Guide**

ROCKS

A Choose just one answer, a, b, c or d.

1 Rock which does not allow water to pass through it is described as
(a) Pervious
(b) Permeable
(c) Porous
(d) Impermeable (1 mark)

2 Which of the following is a metamorphic rock?
(a) Marble
(b) Sandstone
(c) Clay
(d) Granite (1 mark)

3 Which of the following is an igneous rock?
(a) Chalk (b) Basalt
(c) Slate (d) Limestone (1 mark)

4 Which of the following is a sedimentary rock?
(a) Marble (c) Quartzite
(b) Basalt (d) Limestone (1 mark)

5 Which of the following rocks is the hardest?
(a) Slate
(b) Granite
(c) Clay
(d) Sandstone (1 mark)

slate   granite   clay   sandstone

Score /5

B Answer all parts of all questions.

1 Decide whether the statements below are true or false.

True False

(a) Metamorphic rocks are formed from igneous and sedimentary rocks ☐ ☐

(b) Horizontal cracks in sedimentary rocks are called joints ☐ ☐

(c) Cracks in rocks caused by tectonic movements are called faults ☐ ☐

(d) Chalk is formed from the remains of sea creatures ☐ ☐

(e) Clay is formed from the remains of plants ☐ ☐

(f) Granite is an extrusive igneous rock ☐ ☐

(g) Basalt has a fine texture ☐ ☐

(h) Freeze-thaw weathering is a type of chemical weathering ☐ ☐

(i) When water freezes it expands by up to 15% ☐ ☐

(j) All rainwater is acidic ☐ ☐ (10 marks)

Score /10

C

These are GCSE-style questions. Answer all parts of the questions.

1 The photograph below shows Aberfan, Wales, following the collapse of a coal spoil heap in 1966.

(a) Define the term 'mass movement'.

.... (1 mark)

(b) With reference to the photograph, suggest why mass movement can be a hazard for people and property.

....

....

.... (3 marks)

(c) Soil creep is a very slow form of mass movement. What might you look for as evidence of soil creep?

....

.... (2 marks)

(d) Explain the causes of a type of mass movement you have studied.

....

....

....

.... (4 marks)

Score   /10

How well did you do?

0–6 correct   Try again
7–13 correct   Getting there
14–19 correct   Good work
20–25 correct   Excellent!

TOTAL SCORE   **/25**

**For more on this topic
see pages 10–11 of your Success Guide**

LANDFORMS

A

Choose just one answer, a, b, c or d.

1 Which of the following is not a use of limestone?
(a) Building material
(b) Fertiliser
(c) Cement
(d) Pottery   (1 mark)

2 Which of the following is not a surface landform in a limestone area?
(a) Stalactite
(b) Shake hole
(c) Clint
(d) Grike   (1 mark)

3 Which of the following words is not an igneous intrusion?
(a) Sill   (b) Dyke

(c) Tor   (d) Batholith   (1 mark)

4 Which of the following is not a use of granite?
(a) Building material
(b) Pottery
(c) Paint
(d) Fertiliser   (1 mark)

5 Which of the following best describes a granite area?
(a) Upland area with many rivers and marshes
(b) Lowland area with many rivers and marshes
(c) Upland area with few rivers and marshes
(d) Lowland area with few rivers and marshes
                                                (1 mark)

Score   /5

B

Answer all parts of all questions.

1 The diagram below shows a chalk and clay landscape.

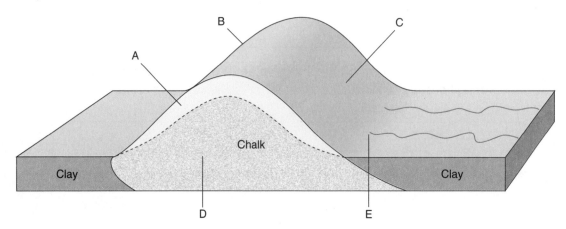

(a) Label features A–E.   (5 marks)

(b) Give four ways in which chalk and clay landscapes are used by people.

....

....

....

.... (4 marks)

Score   /9

C These are GCSE-style questions. Answer all parts of the questions.

1 Study the map, which shows the distribution of limestone, granite, chalk and clay in the British Isles.

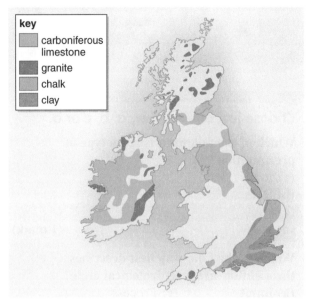

key
- carboniferous limestone
- granite
- chalk
- clay

(a) Describe the distribution of the different rock types shown on the map.

....

....

....

.... (4 marks)

(b) Carboniferous limestone is a hard sedimentary rock which forms a karst landscape. Describe the characteristics of a karst landscape.

....

....

....

.... (4 marks)

(c) Explain the formation of a limestone pavement. You may use diagrams to help you.

....

....

....

....

....

.... (6 marks)

Score   /14

How well did you do?
0–7 correct   Try again
8–14 correct   Getting there
15–21 correct   Good work
22–28 correct   Excellent!

TOTAL SCORE   /28

For more on this topic
see pages 12–13 of your Success Guide

RIVER PROCESSES

A

Choose just one answer, a, b, c or d.

1 Which of the following is not a type of precipitation?
(a) Ice
(b) Rain
(c) Hail
(d) Snow   (1 mark)

2 Which of the following best describes throughflow in the hydrological cycle?
(a) Input   (c) Process
(b) Store   (d) Output   (1 mark)

3 Which of the following best describes groundwater in the hydrological cycle?
(a) Input   (c) Process
(b) Store   (d) Output   (1 mark)

4 Which word describes the process of water turning into water vapour?
(a) Condensation
(b) Precipitation
(c) Interception
(d) Evaporation   (1 mark)

5 Which of the following is not a river process?
(a) Erosion
(b) Transpiration
(c) Transportation
(d) Deposition   (1 mark)

Score   /5

B

Answer all parts of all questions.

1 Complete the following sentences using the words on the right.

(a) .... is the sheer force of the river water on the bed and banks.

| saltation |

(b) .... is caused by stones and pebbles wearing away the river channel.

| corrasion |

(c) .... is when river water dissolves rocks made from calcium carbonate.

| corrosion |

(d) Stones and pebbles in the river are broken down by ....

| solution |

(e) Rocks and boulders in the river are rolled along by ....

| hydraulic power |

(f) Stones and pebbles are bounced along the river bed by ....

| traction |

(g) .... is when fine particles of silt float in the river water.

| suspension |

(h) .... is when minerals have been dissolved in the river water.

| attrition |

(8 marks)

Score   /8

16

C These are GCSE-style questions. Answer all parts of the questions.

1 Study the diagrams below, which show how a river valley changes from the source to the mouth.

Upper course

Middle course

Lower course

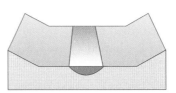

(a) Describe how the shape of the valley changes along the river's course.

....

.... (2 marks)

(b) Describe and explain how you would expect the bedload of the river to change from source to mouth.

....

....

....

.... (4 marks)

(c) Explain why discharge increases as the river flows downstream.

....

.... (2 marks)

(d) Explain why river velocity is expected to increase downstream.

....

....

....

.... (4 marks)

(e) Describe the long profile of a river you have studied.

....

....

.... (3 marks)

Score /15

How well did you do?

0–7 correct   Try again
8–14 correct   Getting there
15–21 correct   Good work
22–28 correct   Excellent!

TOTAL SCORE /28

For more on this topic see pages 14–15 of your Success Guide

RIVER LANDFORMS

A

Choose just one answer, a, b, c or d.

1 Towards the source, the river valley is described as
   (a) U-shaped   (c) W-shaped
   (b) V-shaped   (d) Y-shaped   (1 mark)

2 Interlocking spurs are formed when
   (a) A river begins to meander
   (b) A river increases in velocity
   (c) A river deposits material
   (d) A river enters the sea   (1 mark)

3 Which of the following does not help to form a flood plain?
   (a) Erosion
   (b) Deposition
   (c) Percolation
   (d) Flooding   (1 mark)

4 What is a distributary?
   (a) A large river flowing into the sea
   (b) A small river flowing into a lake
   (c) A small river joining a larger river
   (d) A small river branching away from a larger river   (1 mark)

5 Under which of the following conditions are deltas unlikely to form?
   (a) The river is transporting a large amount of sediment
   (b) The sea has a large tidal range
   (c) The sea has weak currents
   (d) The sea is shallow at the river mouth   (1 mark)

Score   /5

B

Answer all parts of all questions.

1 The diagram shows a simplified river basin.

Label features A–E.

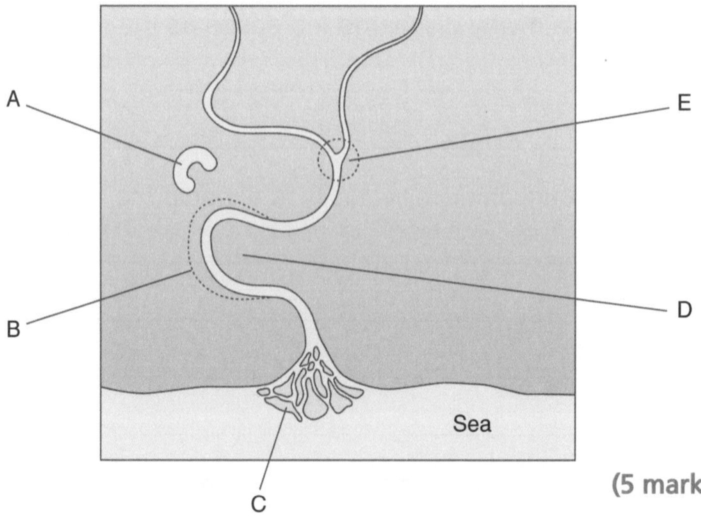

Sea

(5 marks)

2 Decide whether the statements below are true or false.

	True	False
(a) A meander is a curve in a river	☐	☐
(b) The inside bend of a meander is called a river cliff	☐	☐
(c) Meanders migrate slowly downstream	☐	☐
(d) Meanders are found only in the lower course of a river	☐	☐
(e) Rivers flow slowest on the outside bend of a meander	☐	☐

(5 marks)

Score   /10

C **These are GCSE-style questions. Answer all parts of the questions.**

1 Study the photograph, which shows a small waterfall.

(a) Describe the landscape shown in the photograph.

....

....

.... (4 marks)

(b) With reference to an example you have studied, explain the formation of a waterfall.

....

....

....

....

....

.... (6 marks)

2 (a) What is a levée?

.... (2 marks)

(b) Under what conditions do levées form naturally?

....

....

.... (3 marks)

Score   /15

TOTAL SCORE   **/30**

**For more on this topic
see pages 16–17 of your Success Guide**

FLOODING

A

Choose just one answer, a, b, c or d.

1 Which of the following is not a cause of flooding?
(a) Precipitation   (b) Afforestation
(c) Urbanisation   (d) Deforestation
(1 mark)

2 Which of the following conditions results in the shortest lag time?
(a) Gentle slopes and permeable rock
(b) Steep slopes and impermeable rock
(c) Steep slopes and dense vegetation
(d) Gentle slopes and sparse vegetation
(1 mark)

3 Which of the following is a positive impact of flooding?
(a) Silt deposited on farmland

(b) Airports closed
(c) Property submerged
(d) Sewage mixes with floodwater   (1 mark)

4 Which of the following is a soft flood control method?
(a) Dams
(b) Levées
(c) Spillways
(d) Zoning   (1 mark)

5 Which of the following is not a long-term impact of flooding?
(a) People drowned
(b) Buildings damaged
(c) Roads closed
(d) Cost of repairs   (1 mark)

Score   /5

B

Answer all parts of all questions.

1 Study the hydrograph.

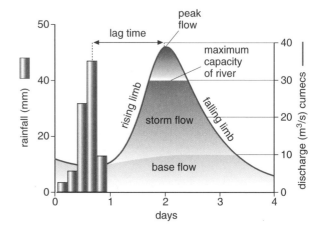

(a) What three variables are shown on a hydrograph? .... (1 mark)

(b) What is meant by the term 'lag time'? ....

.... (1 mark)

(c) What is the lag time shown on the hydrograph? .... (1 mark)

(d) What is the maximum capacity of the river before it will flood?.. (1 mark)

(e) What is the peak flow shown on the hydrograph? .... (1 mark)

Score   /5

C **These are GCSE-style questions. Answer all parts of the questions.**

1 Study the map, which shows details of the floods which affected southern Africa in 2000.

(a) Name the three countries affected by the flooding in southern Africa.

....

....

....

(3 marks)

key

☐ area of floods

Zambezi River

ZIMBABWE

Beira

⊕ Nova Sofala
Red Cross
relief centre

Massangena

Beitbridge Dam

Save River

● Inhassoro
Save the Children
relief centre

BOTSWANA

Limpopo River

MOZAMBIQUE

SOUTH AFRICA

Massingir Dam

● Inhambane

March 2000
More flood waters are moving down the Limpopo and Save Rivers after heavy rains in South Africa and Zimbabwe. Another cyclone is heading for Mozambique from over the Indian Ocean, but meteorologists say it is over a week away and may fizzle out or veer away.

Palmeiras
South African
Defence Force
helicopters
based here

Incomati River

● Chokwe

● Xai-Xai
Town of 130,000
completely submerged

● Maputo

SWAZILAND

0   200 km

(b) What caused the flooding in southern Africa?

.... (2 marks)

(c) Why was Mozambique at risk from further flooding?

.... (2 marks)

(d) What is the distance between the Palmeiras helicopter base and the Red Cross relief centre?

.... (1 mark)

(e) Suggest why the distance between the helicopter base and the relief centre made the relief operation difficult.

.... (1 mark)

(f) Describe the effects of a flood in a less economically developed country that you have studied.

....

....

....

....

....

.... (6 marks)

Score   /15

How well did you do?

0–6 correct   Try again
7–13 correct   Getting there
14–19 correct   Good work
20–25 correct   Excellent!

TOTAL SCORE   /25

For more on this topic
see pages 18–19 of your Success Guide

COASTAL PROCESSES

A Choose just one answer, a, b, c or d.

1 Which of the following describes the distance travelled by a wave?
(a) Wave length
(b) Wave strength
(c) Frequency
(d) Fetch   (1 mark)

2 Which of the following causes waves?
(a) The Earth's gravity
(b) The wind
(c) The moon
(d) Longshore drift   (1 mark)

3 Which of the following are not formed by deposition?
(a) Bays   (b) Beaches
(c) Spits   (d) Sandbars   (1 mark)

4 Which of the following is not a source of beach material?
(a) Cliff
(b) Offshore bank
(c) Sand dune
(d) River   (1 mark)

5 Which of the following types of beach material is the largest?
(a) Cobbles
(b) Silt
(c) Sand
(d) Pebbles   (1 mark)

Score   /5

B Answer all parts of all questions.

1 Match the following descriptions of how beach material is transported with the key words.

(a) Calcium carbonate and salts are dissolved in the water | traction

(b) Sand and silt float in the water | saltation

(c) Cobbles are rolled along by the waves | suspension

(d) Pebbles are bounced along by the waves | solution

(4 marks)

2 Cross out the incorrect words in the sentences below.

(a) Waves break when they approach shallow/deep water.

(b) A wave surging up a beach is called swash/backwash.

(c) Destructive waves occur when they are low/high in proportion to their length.

(d) Constructive waves occur in high/light winds.

(e) A wave frequency of 6 to 9 per minute results in constructive/destructive waves.

(f) Strong swash and weak backwash result in constructive/destructive waves.   (6 marks)

Score   /10

C These are GCSE-style questions. Answer all parts of the questions.

1 Study the photograph of the coast below.

(a) Describe the landscape shown in the photograph.

....

....

....

.... (4 marks)

(b) Describe the conditions which lead to the formation of powerful waves.

....

....

....

.... (4 marks)

(c) With reference to the photograph, suggest how the waves are eroding the cliffs.

....

....

....

....

....

.... (6 marks)

Score /14

How well did you do?
0-7 correct Try again
8-15 correct Getting there
16-22 correct Good work
23-29 correct Excellent!

TOTAL SCORE /29

**For more on this topic
see pages 20–21 of your Success Guide**

23

COASTAL LANDFORMS

A

Choose just one answer, a, b, c or d.

1 Where is the most likely place for a spit to form?
(a) Salt marsh
(b) Cliff
(c) River mouth
(d) Wave-cut platform (1 mark)

2 What is likely to form in the sheltered area behind a spit?
(a) Salt marsh
(b) Hooked end
(c) Sand dunes
(d) Bar (1 mark)

3 What is the word for a ridge running along a beach?
(a) Platform　　(b) Bar
(c) Dune　　(d) Berm (1 mark)

4 Material is moved along a beach by the process of
(a) Longshore erosion
(b) Longshore drift
(c) Longshore transportation
(d) Longshore deposition (1 mark)

5 Which of the following coastal landforms is not formed by erosion?
(a) Beach
(b) Headland
(c) Cliff
(d) Wave-cut platform (1 mark)

Score /5

B

Answer all parts of all questions.

1 Arrange the following statements in the correct order to explain how cliffs and wave-cut platforms are formed.

(a) The cliff becomes unstable, especially when saturated with rainwater. ☐

(b) The cliff collapses under the force of gravity. ☐

(c) The coastline retreats inland to create a wave-cut platform. ☐

(d) The cliff becomes undercut and a wave-cut notch is formed. ☐

(e) Hydraulic pressure and abrasion erode the base of the cliff. ☐ (5 marks)

2 (a) Where would you expect to find a wave-cut notch?
.... (1 mark)

(b) Which type of rock would result in the steepest cliffs – clay or limestone?
.... (1 mark)

(c) Which type of rock would result in the most rapid rate of retreat – granite or sandstone?
.... (1 mark)

Score /8

C These are GCSE-style questions. Answer all parts of the questions.

1 Study the diagram.

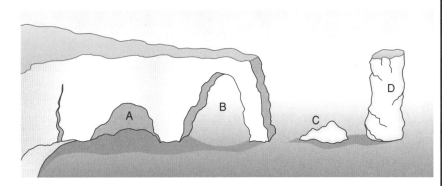

(a) Label landforms A–D. (4 marks)

(b) Name an example of landform D. .... (1 mark)

(c) Explain how landform D was formed. You may use diagrams to help you.

....

....

....

.... (6 marks)

2 The map shows an area of headlands and bays in Dorset.

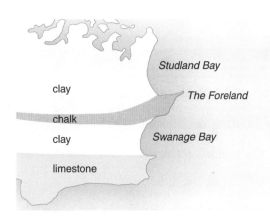

(a) Define the terms 'headland' and 'bay'.

....

.... (2 marks)

(b) Explain how headlands and bays may be formed. ....

....

....

.... (4 marks)

Score   /17

ow well did you do?

-8 correct   Try again
5 correct   Getting there
3 correct   Good work
0 correct   Excellent!

TOTAL SCORE   /30

For more on this topic
see pages 22–23 of your Success Guide

COASTAL MANAGEMENT

A

Choose just one answer, a, b, c or d.

1 Which of the following areas has the greatest need for coastal protection?
(a) Low economic value and low population
(b) High economic value and low population
(c) High economic value and high population
(d) Low economic value and high population
(1 mark)

2 Managed retreat may best be described as
(a) Sea is prevented from flooding and eroding the coast
(b) Sea is prevented from flooding but is allowed to erode the coast
(c) Sea is prevented from eroding but is allowed to flood the coast
(d) Sea is allowed to erode and flood the coast
(1 mark)

3 The cost of coastal protection is paid for by
(a) DEFRA (70%), local authority (30%)
(b) DEFRA (30%), local authority (70%)
(c) DEFRA (50%), local authority (50%)
(d) DEFRA (100%)
(1 mark)

4 Which of the following is not a tourist attraction in coastal areas?
(a) Beaches (b) Sea (c) Waterfalls (d) Cliffs
(1 mark)

5 Which of the following is a disadvantage of tourism in coastal areas?
(a) Employment for local people
(b) Injection of money to local economy
(c) Increase in congestion
(d) Additional recreational facilities (1 mark)

Score   /5

B

Answer all parts of all questions.

1 Match the following descriptions with the correct type of coastal defence.

(a) Sand and pebbles are dredged from the sea bed and

added to existing beaches.

(b) Wooden barriers which extend into the sea are built

across the beach.

(c) Large boulders are placed at the base of cliffs to prevent erosion.

(d) Concrete barriers are built at the back of the beach.

(e) Cobbles and pebbles are wired together in a steel mesh.

(f) Steep slopes are drained and terraced.

gabions

groynes

sea wall

cliff stabilisation

beach nourishment

rock armour

(6 marks)

2 Coastal defences may be described as 'hard' or 'soft' engineering. State one advantage and one disadvantage of each.

Hard engineering ....

Soft engineering .... (4 marks)

Score   /10

C **These are GCSE-style questions. Answer all parts of the questions.**

1 Study the photograph. It shows a landslide which has occured.

(a) Explain why the landslide is likely to have occurred.

....

....

....

.... (4 marks)

(b) Suggest how the owners of the hotel might have been affected by the landslide.

....

.... (2 marks)

(c) Suggest why the area of coastline affected was not protected by coastal defences.

....

....

.... (3 marks)

(d) With reference to a coastal area you have studied, explain how problems resulting from tourism may be managed.

....

....

....

....

....

.... (6 marks)

Score   /15

How well did you do?

0–8 correct   Try again
9–15 correct   Getting there
6–23 correct   Good work
4–30 correct   Excellent!

TOTAL SCORE   /30

For more on this topic see pages 24–25 of your Success Guide

GLACIATION

A **Choose just one answer, a, b, c or d.**

1 When did the most recent glacial period
(ice age) begin?
(a) 10,000 years ago (b) 50,000 years ago
(c) 80,000 years ago (d) 100,000 years ago
(1 mark)

2 During the last glacial period, ice sheets
extended from the north and south poles
to cover
(a) 10% of the planet
(b) 30% of the planet
(c) 70% of the planet
(d) 100% of the planet
(1 mark)

3 The current interglacial period began when
the ice sheets retreated
(a) 10,000 years ago

(b) 50,000 years ago
(c) 80,000 years ago
(d) 100,000 years ago
(1 mark)

4 In which of the following locations would you
find an ice sheet today?
(a) Alps
(b) Rockies
(c) Himalayas
(d) Antarctica
(1 mark)

5 Ice sheets can be up to
(a) 35 metres thick
(b) 350 metres thick
(c) 3,500 metres thick
(d) 35,000 metres thick
(1 mark)

Score   /5

B **Answer all parts of all questions.**

1 Match the following descriptions with the correct glacial process below.

(a) Glacier retreats due to melting ....

(b) Glacier extends as more snow falls ....

(c) Glacier bends and flows as ice crystals slide past each other ....

(d) Glacier slides over meltwater beneath its base ....

(e) Glacier pulls away loose rocks ....

| plucking |
| ablation |
| slippage |
| accumulation |
| deformation |

(5 marks)

2 Arrange the following statements in the correct order to explain how glaciers are formed.

(a) Glacier begins to slide downhill due to gravity. ☐

(b) Snow falls in upland areas. ☐

(c) Firn is compressed to form ice. ☐

(d) Layers of snow build up over many years. ☐

(e) Snow is compressed to form firn. ☐

(5 marks)

Score   /10

C These are GCSE-style questions. Answer all parts of the questions.

1 Study the diagram, which shows a glaciated valley in the Alps.

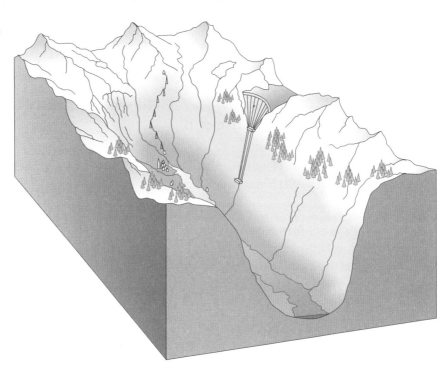

(a) Describe the human uses of upland glaciated areas using the following categories.

Farming ....

Communications ....

Tourism .... (6 marks)

(b) Explain why upland glaciated areas provide excellent opportunities for producing

hydroelectric power (HEP). ....

.... (2 marks)

(c) Explain why settlement is limited in upland glaciated areas.

....

.... (2 marks)

(d) With reference to an example you have studied, describe the problems caused by

tourism in upland glaciated areas. ....

....

....

.... (4 marks)

Score   /14

How well did you do?
0–7 correct   Try again
8–15 correct   Getting there
16–22 correct   Good work
23–29 correct   Excellent!

TOTAL SCORE   /29

For more on this topic see pages 26–27 of your Success Guide

GLACIAL LANDFORMS

A

Choose just one answer, a, b, c or d.

1 Glaciers erode a deep
(a) V-shaped valley (b) U-shaped valley
(c) W-shaped valley (d) Y-shaped valley
(1 mark)

2 Hanging valleys are formed where
(a) A river flows into a ribbon lake
(b) Moraine is deposited across the valley floor
(c) A smaller glacier joins a larger glacier
(d) A waterfall erodes a small gorge (1 mark)

3 Truncated spurs are formed when
(a) A glacier melts and deposits eroded material
(b) A glacier cracks on its surface
(c) A glacier follows the original river meanders
(d) A glacier erodes the hills either side of the valley (1 mark)

4 A ribbon lake is
(a) A long narrow lake on the valley floor
(b) A short narrow lake on the valley floor
(c) A long narrow lake below the mountain summit
(d) A short wide lake below the mountain summit (1 mark)

5 Crevasses are formed when
(a) A glacier expands as it freezes
(b) A glacier passes over the corrie lip
(c) A glacier contracts as it melts
(d) A glacier erodes its base (1 mark)

Score /5

B

Answer all parts of all questions.

1 The diagram shows different types of moraine.

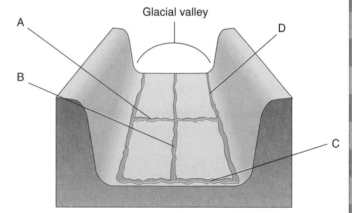

Glacial valley

A
B
C
D

(a) What is moraine? ....
.... (2 marks)

(b) Label the four different types of moraine A–D on the diagram. (4 marks)

(c) Suggest a reason for the location of each type of moraine.

A ....

B ....

C ....

D .... (4 marks)

Score /10

C These are GCSE-style questions. Answer all parts of the questions.

1 Study the diagram of an upland glaciated area below.

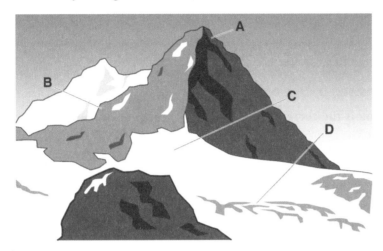

(a) Identify landforms A–D on the diagram.

....

....

.... (4 marks)

(b) Name an example of landform A. .... (1 mark)

(c) Explain how landform A is formed. You may use diagrams to help you.

....

....

....

....

....

.... (6 marks)

2 (a) What is a drumlin? ....

.... (1 mark)

(b) Explain how drumlins may be formed. ....

....

....

.... (3 marks)

Score   /15

How well did you do?

0–8 correct   Try again
9–15 correct   Getting there
16–23 correct   Good work
24–30 correct   Excellent!

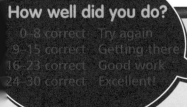

TOTAL SCORE   /30

For more on this topic
see pages 28–29 of your Success Guide

31

WEATHER

A **Choose just one answer, a, b, c or d.**

1 Which of the following is the correct definition of 'weather'?
(a) The average atmospheric conditions of a place
(b) The atmospheric conditions at a certain place and time
(c) The average atmospheric conditions at a certain place and time
(d) The atmospheric conditions of a climate
(1 mark)

2 Which of the following is a warm front?
(a)
(b)
(c)
(d)
(1 mark)

3 Which of the following are used to show air pressure on a synoptic chart?
(a) Isohels (b) Isohyets
(c) Isobars (d) Isotherms (1 mark)

4 Which of the following is not a measure of wind speed?
(a) Knots (b) Km/hour
(c) Beaufort scale (d) Mercalli scale
(1 mark)

5 Which of the following best describes an anticyclone in winter?
(a) Light winds, clouds and rain
(b) High winds, sunshine and frost
(c) Light winds, sunshine and frost
(d) High winds, cloud and rain (1 mark)

Score /5

B **Answer all parts of all questions.**

1 Match the types of weather below with the instruments used to measure them.

(a) Temperature ....

(b) Air pressure ....

(c) Wind speed ....

(d) Humidity ....

(e) Precipitation ....

barometer

wet-and-dry bulb thermometer

rain gauge

thermometer

anemometer

(5 marks)

2 Arrange the following statements in the correct order to explain how convectional rainfall happens.

(a) Water droplets combine to form rain drops. ☐
(b) Solar energy heats the Earth's surface. ☐
(c) Air cools and condenses. ☐
(d) Air is warmed and begins to rise. ☐
(e) Clouds form. ☐

(5 marks)

Score /10

32

C These are GCSE-style questions. Answer all parts of the questions.

1 Study the satellite image of a depression.

(a) Label A–D on the satellite image. (4 marks)

(b) In which direction do depressions rotate in the northern hemisphere?

....

.... (1 mark)

D

A   B   C

2 Study the cross-section of a depression below.

Warm sector

Cool air mass

Cool air mass

London

Depression moving eastwards

(a) Describe how the weather in London is likely to change during the next 24 hours.

....

....

....

....

.... (5 marks)

(b) Explain how a depression forms. You may use diagrams to help you.

....

....

....

....

.... (5 marks)

Score   /15

How well did you do?

0–8 correct   Try again
9–15 correct   Getting there
16–23 correct   Good work
24–30 correct   Excellent!

TOTAL SCORE   /30

For more on this topic
see pages 30–31 of your Success Guide

33

CLIMATE

Choose just one answer, a, b, c or d.

1 Climate is the average weather of a place based on data collected over a
(a) 3-year period   (b) 30-year period
(c) 100-year period   (d) 300-year period
(1 mark)

2 If the temperature is 10°C at sea level, what will the temperature be 2,000 metres up a mountain?
(a) 2°C   b) 0°C
(c) –2°C   d) –4°C   (1 mark)

3 What is the climate type of the UK?
(a) Temperate maritime
(b) Mediterranean
(c) Continental interior
(d) Tropical   (1 mark)

4 What is the average temperature in London during the summer?
(a) 7°C
(b) 10°C
(c) 15°C
(d) 17°C   (1 mark)

5 Which of the following climate types are not found in Australia?
(a) Desert
(b) Tundra
(c) Tropical grassland
(d) Tropical   (1 mark)

Score   /5

Answer all parts of all questions.

1 Decide whether the statements below are true or false.

                                                      True   False

(a) Solar energy is concentrated at the equator   ☐   ☐

(b) Temperature increases with altitude   ☐   ☐

(c) Polar winds bring cold weather   ☐   ☐

(d) Places that are influenced by the sea have a continental climate   ☐   ☐

(e) Cold ocean currents can cause fog   ☐   ☐   (5 marks)

2 Match the descriptions below to the correct climate type.

(a) Hot all year with a wet season and a dry season | tropical |

(b) Hot all year with very little rain | desert |

(c) Moderate temperatures and rain all year | temperate maritime |

(d) Hot and wet all year | tropical grassland |

(e) Hot dry summers and mild wet winters | Mediterranean |

(5 marks)

Score   /10

C **These are GCSE-style questions. Answer all parts of the questions.**

1 Study the map on the right, which shows the average temperatures for the British Isles during January.

key

⁓ isotherm

January temperatures

(a) Which are the warmest areas during January?

....

.... (2 marks)

(b) Which are the coldest areas during January?

....

.... (2 marks)

4°C

4°C

5°C

6°C

7°C

(c) Give two reasons to explain the pattern of temperatures in January.

....

....

....

.... (4 marks)

2 Study the map on the right, which shows the annual precipitation in the British Isles.

key

▓ over 2,000 mm

☐ 750–2,000 mm

☐ under 750 mm

Annual precipitation

(a) Name the wettest place identified on the map.

.... (1 mark)

(b) Name the driest place identified on the map.

.... (1 mark)

• Inverness 730 mm

Fort William • 2,000 mm

Glasgow 1,560 mm

Keswick • 1,480 mm

• Newcastle 630 mm

(c) Describe the general pattern of precipitation shown on the map.

....

....(2 marks)

• Manchester 860 mm

Aberystwyth • 934 mm

Norwich 650 mm

London 610 mm

Falmouth • 1,100 mm

(d) Explain the pattern of precipitation shown on the map.

....

....

.... (3 marks)

Score   /15

How well did you do?

0–8 correct   Try again
9–15 correct   Getting there
16–23 correct   Good work
24–30 correct   Excellent!

TOTAL SCORE   /30

For more on this topic
see pages 32–33 of your Success Guide

WEATHER AND PEOPLE

A — Choose just one answer, a, b, c or d.

1 Which of the following is not a name for a tropical storm?
(a) Tornado   (b) Hurricane
(c) Cyclone   (d) Typhoon   (1 mark)

2 Hurricanes may form when sea temperatures reach
(a) 26°C   (b) 27°C
(c) 28°C   (d) 29°C   (1 mark)

3 How large do tropical storms grow?
(a) 5 km across
(b) 50 km across
(c) 500 km across
(d) 5,000 km across   (1 mark)

4 How long do tropical storms usually last?
(a) One to two days
(b) One to seven days
(c) Seven to ten days
(d) Seven to fourteen days   (1 mark)

5 Which of the following is not an impact of hurricanes?
(a) Drought
(b) Flooding
(c) Landslides
(d) Storm surge   (1 mark)

Score /5

B — Answer all parts of all questions.

1 (a) What is a drought? .... (1 mark)

(b) Name an area affected by drought. .... (1 mark)

(c) What proportion of the world's population live in areas at risk of drought? .... (1 mark)

(d) How do people help to cause droughts? .... (2 marks)

2 Arrange the following statements in the correct order to explain the physical causes of drought.

(a) Air sinks and warms up. ☐

(b) An area of high pressure develops. ☐

(c) Warm air is able to hold more water vapour. ☐

(d) Warm dry winds blow outwards blocking any depressions. ☐

(e) Clouds evaporate. ☐   (5 marks)

Score /10

C These are GCSE-style questions. Answer all parts of the questions.

1 Study the map, which shows details of Hurricane Mitch.

Hurricane Mitch became the Atlantics basin's fourth-strongest hurricame ever, claiming thousands of lives in Central America.

Mexico
6 dead
thousands
evacuated

Belize
thousands
evacuated

Honduras
14,000 dead
70% of crops
destroyed

Path of hurricane

Atlantic Ocean

22 Sept 1998
Hurricane
Mitch begins

Guatemala
28 bridges destroyed
440 dead

El Salvador
50% of crops destroyed
370 dead
50,000 homeless

Costa Rica

Nicaragua
3,500 dead
725,000 homeless
60% with no electricity

Panama

(a) Describe the route taken by Hurricane Mitch.

....

....

.... (4 marks)

(b) Describe the impact of the hurricane on people.

....

....

.... (4 marks)

(c) Suggest why Hurricane Mitch caused so much death and destruction.

....

....

....

.... (4 marks)

(d) Explain how Hurricane Mitch was formed. You may use diagrams to help you.

....

....

....

....

....

.... (6 marks)

Score   /18

How well did you do?

0–8 correct   Try again
9–17 correct   Getting there
18–25 correct   Good work
26–33 correct   Excellent!

TOTAL SCORE   /33

**For more on this topic
see pages 34–35 of your Success Guide**

POPULATION

A

Choose just one answer, a, b, c or d.

1 What is the approximate total global population today?
(a) 6 million people
(b) 600 million people
(c) 6 billion people *(circled)*
(d) 60 billion people   (1 mark)

2 When did the global population reach 1 billion?
(a) 1700   **(b)** 1800 *(circled)*
(c) 1900   (d) 2000   (1 mark)

3 The rapid growth in population during the last 200 years is called the
(a) Population explosion *(circled)*
(b) Population contraction
(c) Population implosion
(d) Population distribution   (1 mark)

4 What percentage of the total global population growth is taking place in LEDCs?
(a) 35%
(b) 50%
(c) 75% *(circled)*
(d) 95%   (1 mark)

5 The global population is predicted to stabilise in 2200 at
(a) 8.7 billion
(b) 9.2 billion
(c) 10.4 billion *(circled)*
(d) 12.6 billion   (1 mark)

Score   /5

B

Answer all parts of all questions.

1 (a) Calculate the population density for each of the countries in the table below.   (5 marks)

Country	Population (millions)	Area (km²)	Population density (per km²)
UK	60	245,000	
France	59	545,000	
Australia	20	7,618,000	
USA	287	9,100,000	
China	1,280	9,326,000	

(b) Which country is the most crowded?

.... (1 mark)

2 (a) Define the term 'birth rate'.

No. of births per 1,000 per year   (1 mark)

(b) Define the term 'death rate'.

No. of deaths per 1,000 per year   (1 mark)

(c) Define the term 'natural increase in population'.

BR – DR   Increase in pop. if greater than DR   (1 mark)

Score   /9

These are GCSE-style questions. Answer all parts of the questions.

POPULATION

1 Study the map, which shows population density around the world.

(a) Describe the distribution of areas of high population density.

Areas are mainly
Europe, Asia
and East, West
America

(2 marks)

key
people per km^2

 above 50

 10 to 50

 fewer than 10

(b) Describe the distribution of areas of low population density.

....

.... (2 marks)

(c) Suggest reasons for the patterns you have described in **(a)** and **(b)**.

....

....

....

.... (4 marks)

(d) Name an area of the UK with a high population density.

....
(1 mark)

(e) Explain why the area you named in **(d)** has a high population density.

....

....

.... (3 marks)

(f) Explain how governments collect information about populations.

....

....

.... (3 marks)

Score   /15

How well did you do?

 0–7 correct   Try again
 8–15 correct   Getting there
16–22 correct   Good work
23–29 correct   Excellent!

TOTAL SCORE   /29

**For more on this topic
see pages 42–43 of your Success Guide**

CHANGING POPULATIONS

HUMAN GEOGRAPHY

A Choose just one answer, a, b, c or d.

1 At which stage of the demographic transition model is India?
(a) Stage 1   (b) Stage 2
(c) Stage 3   (d) Stage 4   (1 mark)

2 At which stage of the demographic transition model is Japan?
(a) Stage 1   (b) Stage 2
(c) Stage 3   (d) Stage 4   (1 mark)

3 Which of the following does not explain why people in LEDCs may have many children?
(a) Children help to provide family income
(b) Poor healthcare means not all children survive
(c) Children support their parents in old age
(d) Contraception is freely available   (1 mark)

4 In China a law limits the number of babies per couple. How many babies are they allowed?
(a) One
(b) Two
(c) Three
(d) Four   (1 mark)

5 Which of the following is an advantage of the Chinese policy?
(a) Population growth is slowing down
(b) There are more males than females
(c) Some female babies are abandoned
(d) The population is ageing   (1 mark)

Score   /5

B Answer all parts of all questions.

1 Match the following descriptions of population growth with the correct stage of the demographic transition model.

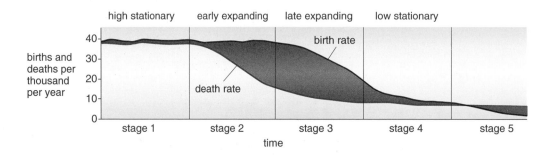

(a) No increase or decrease in population — Stage 1

(b) Very slow increase in population .... Stage 2

(c) Decrease in population .... Stage 3

(d) Rapid increase in population .... Stage 4

(e) Slow increase in population .... Stage 5   (5 marks)

Score   /5

40

C **These are GCSE-style questions. Answer all parts of the questions.**

1 Study the population pyramid graphs below, which show the population structures of India and Japan.

India

male   female

60 50 40 30 20 10 0   0 10 20 30 40 50 60
population (millions)

80+
75-79
70-74
65-69
60-64
55-59
50-54
45-49
40-44
35-39
30-34
25-29
20-24
15-19
10-14
5-9
0-4

Japan

male   female

60 50 40 30 20 10 0   0 10 20 30 40 50 60
population (millions)

95-99
90-94
85-89
80-84
75-79
70-74
65-69
60-64
55-59
50-54
45-49
40-44
35-39
30-34
25-29
20-24
15-19
10-14
5-9
0-4

(a) What information is shown by a population pyramid graph?

....

....

.... (3 marks)

(b) Describe the population pyramid for India.

....

....

.... (3 marks)

(c) Suggest reasons to explain the shape of India's population pyramid.

....

....

.... (3 marks)

(d) Describe the population pyramid for Japan.

....

....

.... (3 marks)

(e) Suggest reasons to explain the shape of Japan's population pyramid.

....

....

.... (3 marks)

Score   /15

How well did you do?

0–6 correct   Try again
7–13 correct   Getting there
14–19 correct Good work
20–25 correct Excellent!

TOTAL SCORE   /25

For more on this topic
see pages 44–45 of your Success Guide

HUMAN GEOGRAPHY

MIGRATION

A Choose just one answer, a, b, c or d.

1 Which of the following words best describes the movement of people out of a country?
(a) Emigration (b) Immigration
(c) Migration (d) Deportation (1 mark)

2 Which of the following describes the movement of people from the countryside to cities?
(a) Urban-to-rural migration
(b) Rural-to-urban migration
(c) Rural migration
(d) Urban migration (1 mark)

3 Which of the following describes the movement of people from cities to the countryside?
(a) Urbanisation (b) Counter-urbanisation
(c) Ruralisation (d) Depopulation (1 mark)

4 Approximately how many Mexicans migrate to the USA each year?
(a) 1 million
(b) 2 million
(c) 3 million
(d) 4 million (1 mark)

5 What is the length of the border between the USA and Mexico?
(a) 500 km
(b) 1,000 km
(c) 2,000 km
(d) 4,000 km (1 mark)

Score /5

B Answer all parts of all questions.

1 Give an example of each of the following types of migration.

(a) Internal ....

(b) International ....

(c) Temporary ....

(d) Voluntary ....

(e) Forced .... (5 marks)

2 State whether the following are 'push' or 'pull' factors. Push Pull

(a) A volcano erupts in Montserrat ☐ ☐

(b) A drought occurs in Ethiopia ☐ ☐

(c) Gold is discovered in Siberia ☐ ☐

(d) War breaks out in Iraq ☐ ☐

(e) There is a shortage of skilled workers in the UK ☐ ☐ (5 marks)

Score /10

42

C

These are GCSE-style questions. Answer all parts of the questions.

1 Study the map, which shows the home countries of the world's refugees between 1997 and 2001.

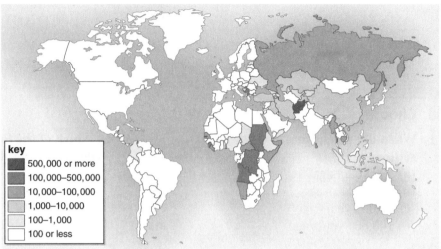

key
500,000 or more
100,000–500,000
10,000–100,000
1,000–10,000
100–1,000
100 or less

(a) What is a refugee?

.... (1 mark)

(b) How many refugees do the United Nations estimate there to be worldwide?

.... (1 mark)

(c) Describe the distribution of refugees' home countries shown on the map.

....

....

....

.... (4 marks)

(d) Suggest reasons to explain the pattern shown on the map.

....

....

....

.... (4 marks)

(e) Describe the causes and consequences of a refugee situation you have studied.

....

....

....

.... (5 marks)

Score   /15

How well did you do?

0–8 correct   Start again
9–15 correct   Getting there
16–23 correct   Good work
24–30 correct   Excellent!

TOTAL SCORE   /30

**For more on this topic
see pages 46–47 of your Success Guide**

MIGRATION

SETTLEMENT

A

Choose just one answer, a, b, c or d.

1 When did people first begin to build settlements?
(a) 500 years ago
(b) 1,000 years ago
(c) 10,000 years ago
(d) 100,000 years ago   (1 mark)

2 Which term best describes the exact location of a settlement?
(a) Hierarchy   (b) Situation
(c) Location   (d) Site   (1 mark)

3 Which of the following site factors remains the most important today?
(a) Fuel   (b) Water
(c) Defence   (d) Transport   (1 mark)

4 Which of the following is not used to determine a settlement hierarchy?
(a) Population
(b) Size
(c) Services
(d) Distance from other settlements   (1 mark)

5 Which term best describes the most important social and economic activities of a settlement?
(a) Range
(b) Socio-economics
(c) Function
(d) Services   (1 mark)

Score   /5

B

Answer all parts of all questions.

1 Complete the following sentences about site and situation using the words on the right.

(a) A supply of .... is needed for building material.

(b) A .... supply is needed to irrigate crops.

(c) A fertile .... is needed to grow crops.

(d) A supply of .... is needed as fuel for cooking and heating.

(e) A .... is needed to provide a good site for defence.

| water |
| timber |
| soil |
| rock |
| river |

(5 marks)

2 Arrange the following settlements in rank order. The most important is number 1, and the least important number 5.

(a) Mega-city ☐
(b) Hamlet ☐
(c) Town ☐
(d) Village ☐
(e) City ☐

(5 marks)

Score   /10

44

These are GCSE-style questions. Answer all parts of the questions.

1 Study the diagram on the right, which shows different settlement patterns.

   (a) Name the type of settlement at A–D.

   A...

   B...

   C...

   D... (4 marks)

2 Study the map below, which shows the sphere of influence of shops in and around Sheffield.

   (a) What is meant by the term 'sphere of influence'?

   ....

   ....

   ....

   ....

   (1 mark)

   Suburban shopping centre

   CBD

   Hypermarket

   Corner shop   Department store

   City Boundary

   Sphere of Influence
   - corner shop
   - suburban shopping centre
   - hypermarket
   - department store

   (b) Describe the sphere of influence of the hypermarket?

   ....

   .... (2 marks)

   (c) Suggest reasons to explain your answer to **(b)**.

   ....

   ....

   ....

   .... (4 marks)

   (d) Explain why the sphere of influence of the corner shop is relatively small.

   ....

   ....

   ....

   .... (4 marks)

   Score   /15

How well did you do?

   0–8 correct   Try again
   9–15 correct   Getting there
   16–23 correct   Good work
   24–30 correct   Excellent!

   TOTAL SCORE   /30

   For more on this topic see pages 48–49 of your Success Guide

SETTLEMENT IN MEDCS

A

Choose just one answer, a, b, c or d.

1 In MEDCs, what is the average percentage of the population living in urban areas?
(a) 30%   (b) 50%
(c) 70%   (d) 90%   (1 mark)

2 Which term best describes the increase in the percentage of people living in cities?
(a) Urbanisation
(b) Urban growth
(c) Urban regeneration
(d) Suburbanisation   (1 mark)

3 How many new homes are needed in England by 2016?
(a) 3 million   (b) 3.4 million
(c) 4 million   (d) 4.4 million   (1 mark)

4 What percentage of new homes does the government want to build on brownfield sites?
(a) 50%
(b) 60%
(c) 70%
(d) 80%   (1 mark)

5 Approximately how many empty buildings are there in England?
(a) One thousand
(b) One million
(c) Five million
(d) Ten million   (1 mark)

Score   /5

B

Answer all parts of all questions.

1 (a) Identify the five land use zones shown on the concentric circle land use model below.

A ....

B ....

C ....

D ....

E .... (5 marks)

(b) Give two reasons to explain the location of the zones you have identified above.

....

....

....

....

....

.... (2 marks)

Score   /7

C

These are GCSE-style questions. Answer all parts of the questions.

1 Study the map, which shows the number of new homes which will be needed in England by 2016.

key
number of new homes needed

■	more than 200,000
■	150,000–199,999
■	100,000–149,999
■	50,000–99,999
□	0–49,999

(a) Give three reasons why more homes are needed in the UK.

....

....

....

....

(3 marks)

(b) Describe the pattern of demand for new housing shown by the map.

....

....

....

....

....

(4 marks)

(c) Suggest why some areas need more homes than others.

....

....

....

.... (4 marks)

(d) Why do developers prefer to build on greenfield sites?

....

.... (2 marks)

(e) Why does the government want most new homes to be built on brownfield sites?

....

.... (2 marks)

Score   /15

How well did you do?

0–7 correct   Try again
8–14 correct   Getting there
5–20 correct   Good work
1–27 correct   Excellent!

TOTAL SCORE   /27

For more on this topic
see pages 50–51 of your Success Guide

SETTLEMENT IN LEDCS

A **Choose just one answer, a, b, c or d.**

1 How many 'million' cities are there in the world?
(a) 100
(b) 200
(c) 300
(d) 400 (1 mark)

2 Which is the largest city in the world?
(a) Moscow
(b) Bombay
(c) Mexico City
(d) Tokyo (1 mark)

3 What is the population of New York?
(a) 17 million people
(b) 20 million people
(c) 23 million people
(d) 25 million people (1 mark)

4 What percentage of people in LEDCs live in urban areas?
(a) 10%
(b) 20%
(c) 30%
(d) 40% (1 mark)

5 Which of the following is a 'push' factor causing urbanisation in LEDCs?
(a) Paid employment
(b) Poor harvests
(c) Good healthcare
(d) Good education (1 mark)

Score /5

B **Answer all parts of all questions.**

1 (a) Identify the five land use zones shown on the LEDC land use model.

(5 marks)

A ....

B ....

C ....

D ....

E ....

(b) Give two differences between a land use model for an MEDC and a land use model for an LEDC.

....

.... (2 marks)

Score /7

48

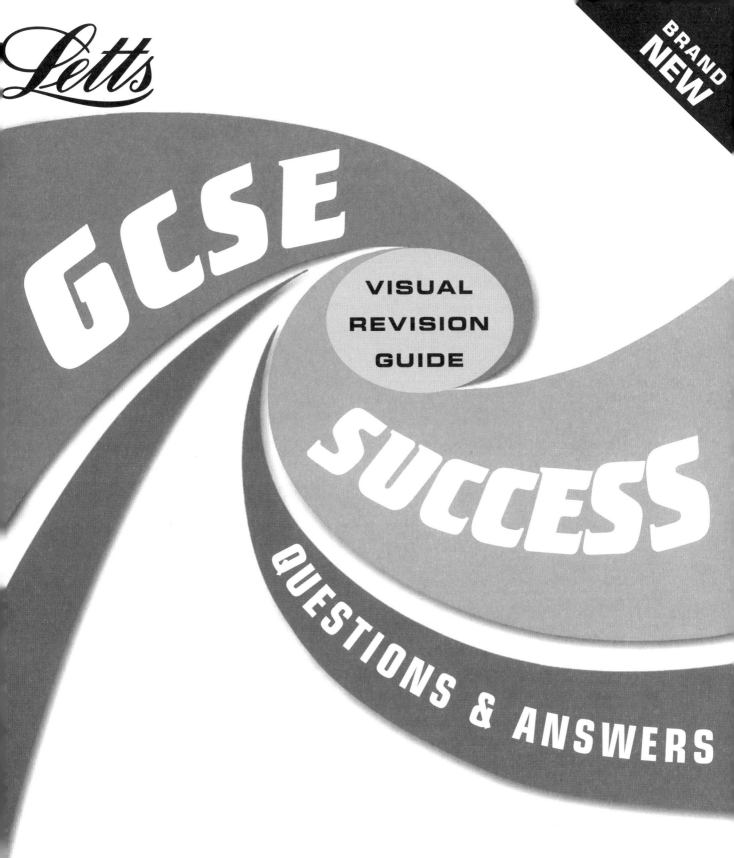

GCSE SUCCESS

VISUAL REVISION GUIDE

QUESTIONS & ANSWERS

BRAND NEW

GEOGRAPHY

Adam Arnell

ANSWER BOOK

TECTONIC ACTIVITY

Section A
1 (c)
2 (b)
3 (d)
4 (d)
5 (c)

Section B
1 (a) Diverging
   (b) Oceanic
   (c) Collision
   (d) Earthquakes
   (e) Continental
   (f) Constructive
2 (a) e.g. Mid-Atlantic Ridge, Iceland
   (b) e.g. Japan
   (c) e.g. India
   (d) e.g. San Andreas Fault, California

Section C
1 (a) Jigsaw fit of continents (1), earthquakes (1), volcanoes (1)
   (b) Earth's core very hot (1), due to radioactive processes (1), heat causes convection currents in mantle (1), movements in mantle drag tectonic plates (1)
   (c) *Level 1* (1–2) basic description of location of earthquakes or volcanoes, *Level 2* (3–4) clearly describes location of earthquakes and volcanoes, noting that they occur in similar areas, *Level 3* (5–6) detailed explanation of location of earthquakes and volcanoes in relation to plate boundaries, noting that volcanoes only occur on some plate boundaries

EARTHQUAKES

Section A
1 (c)
2 (b)
3 (d)
4 (c)
5 (b)

Section B
1 (a) Weighted pen suspended from a frame (1), draws line on roll of paper (1), ground shakes – paper moves from side to side (1), draws waves on paper (1)
   (b) Shock wave caused by earthquake
   (c) P-wave
   (d) S-wave
   (e) 30–40 seconds

Section C
1 (a) (i) Natural environment = hills outside Izmit raised 0.6 metre (1), south of Izmit land moved 4.5 metres to the west (1)
       (ii) People = Izmit: hundreds killed and thousands injured (1), Golcuk: 20 sailors dead and over 100 missing (1), Istanbul: over 100 killed (1)
   (b) Pressure built up at plate boundary (1), movement prevented by friction (1), crust snaps along fault line (1), plates suddenly move (1), stored energy is released as seismic waves (1)
   (c) *Level 1* (1–2) basic suggestions, e.g. stronger buildings, *Level 2* (3–4) clear suggestions, e.g. explains how buildings may be made to withstand earthquakes, *Level 3* (5–6) detailed suggestions which recognise that Turkey has limited funds, e.g. reinforce buildings where possible, emergency plans and earthquake drills

VOLCANOES

Section A
1 (c)
2 (b)
3 (b)
4 (d)
5 (a)

Section B
1 Shield = Mt Etna
   Composite = Mt St Helens
   Hotspot = Mauna Loa
2 (a) Lava flow
   (b) Pyroclastic flow
   (c) Mud flow
   (d) Ash fall

Section C
1 (a) Buildings covered by ash (1), town is deserted (1)
   (b) Montserrat is on a destructive plate boundary (1), South American plate is being forced beneath Caribbean plate (1), crust melts in the mantle (1), magma rises and erupts as a volcano at the surface (1)
   (c) Named volcanic eruption (1), area becomes uninhabitable (1), collapse of agriculture/industry (1), vegetation/coral dies (1), refugees created (1)
   (d) *Level 1* (1–2) basic description, e.g. seismometers and gas sensors used, *Level 2* (3–4) clear explanation, e.g. seismometers record magma chamber filling with lava, *Level 3* (5–6) detailed explanation linked to prediction, e.g. satellites monitor temperature of volcano, increase in temperature suggests volcano is filling with magma and likely to erupt in near future

ROCKS

Section A
1 (d)
2 (a)
3 (b)
4 (d)
5 (b)

Section B
1 (a) True
   (b) False
   (c) True
   (d) True
   (e) False
   (f) False
   (g) True
   (h) False
   (i) False
   (j) True

Section C
1 (a) Rock or soil moving down a slope
   (b) Rapid mass movement may kill or injure people (1) and damage or destroy property (1). This is a hazard both at the top and bottom of a slope (1)
   (c) Bent trees and fences (1), terracettes (1)
   (d) Named example, e.g. Aberfan (1), hill saturated by rainwater (1), rock weakened (1), material slides down slope under force of gravity (1)

LANDFORMS

Section A
1 (d)
2 (a)
3 (d)
4 (d)
5 (a)

Section B
1 (a) A = Scarp slope
       B = Escarpment
       C = Dip slope
       D = Water table
       E = Spring
   (b) Settlement (1), water source (1), animal farming (1), arable farming (1), clay pits (1)

Section C
1 (a) Limestone = Ireland and north-west England (1), granite = Scotland, Ireland and south-west England (1), chalk = south-east England (1), clay = south-east England (1)
   (b) Mountainous area (1), steep slopes (1), exposed rock (1), lack of surface drainage (1), lack of vegetation (1), limestone pavements (1)
   (c) *Level 1* (1–2) describes what a limestone pavement looks like, *Level 2* (3–4) explains how acidic rainwater dissolves limestone to form clints and grikes, *Level 3* (5–6) detailed explanation including why rainwater is acidic or why limestone is well jointed

RIVER PROCESSES

Section A
1 (a)
2 (c)
3 (b)
4 (d)
5 (b)

Section B
1 (a) Hydraulic power
   (b) Corrasion
   (c) Corrosion
   (d) Attrition
   (e) Traction
   (f) Saltation
   (g) Suspension
   (h) Solution

Section C
1 (a) Upper course = narrow and V-shaped (1), lower course = wide and flat (1), Must relate to valley, not river
   (b) Rounder (1), smaller (1), due to erosion (1), by attrition (1)
   (c) Water is added by tributaries (1) and throughflow/groundwater flow (1)
   (d) *Level 1* (1–2) basic description, e.g. less friction from the bed and banks, *Level 2* (3–4) clear explanation, e.g. friction is reduced due to changing ratio between wetted perimeter (bed and banks) and cross-sectional area of river
   (e) Named river (1), concave shape (1), steep to gentle gradient (1)

RIVER LANDFORMS

Section A
1 (b)
2 (a)
3 (c)
4 (d)
5 (b)

Section B
1 A = Ox-bow lake
   B = Meander
   C = Delta
   D = Flood plain
   E = Confluence
2 (a) True
   (b) False
   (c) True
   (d) False
   (e) False

Section C
1 (a) River (1), white water (1), rocks (1), vegetarian/grass (1), valley (1), steep gradient (1)
   (b) *Level 1* (1–2) basic answer, no example, mainly descriptive, *Level 2* (3–4) clear answer, named example, explains different rates of erosion of harder and softer rock, *Level 3* (5–6) detailed answer, named example, explains different rates of erosion using correct terminology in logical sequence, understands that process is repeated many times as waterfall retreats upstream
2 (a) Raised bank either side of river (1), may be natural feature, or a manmade flood defence (1)
   (b) River floods on to flood plain (1), loss of velocity causes river to deposit material (1), largest material is deposited first (1), forming raised banks along side of river (1)

FLOODING

Section A
1 (b)
2 (b)
3 (a)
4 (d)
5 (c)

Section B
1 (a) Rainfall, time, discharge
   (b) Time between peak rainfall and peak discharge
   (c) Approximately 30 hours
   (d) 30 cubic metres per second
   (e) 39 cubic metres per second

Section C
1 (a) Zimbabwe (1), Botswana (1), Mozambique (1)
   (b) Heavy rains (1), caused by a cyclone (1)
   (c) More water is flowing down the Limpopo and Save Rivers (1) and another cyclone is coming (1)
   (d) Approximately 600 km
   (e) Took a long time to distribute emergency supplies due to flying time between helicopter base and relief centre (1)
   (f) *Level 1* (1–2) no named example in LEDC, basic description, e.g. people drowned and houses flooded, *Level 2* (3–4) named example in LEDC, clear description, e.g. one million people homeless and 400 dead, *Level 3* (5–6) named and well located example in LEDC, detailed description of effects with some classification such as physical/human or short-term/long-term

COASTAL PROCESSES

Section A
1 (d)
2 (b)
3 (a)
4 (c)
5 (a)

Section B
1 (a) Solution
   (b) Suspension
   (c) Traction
   (d) Saltation
2 (a) Shallow
   (b) Swash
   (c) High
   (d) Light
   (e) Constructive
   (f) Constructive

Section C
1 (a) Steep cliffs (1), rocky (1), large waves (1), spray (1), trees/vegetation (1), stump/wave-cut platform (1)
   (b) Large fetch (1), strong wind (1), wind blows for a long time (1), steep offshore gradient (1)
   (c) *Level 1* (1–2) basic description about waves breaking up the cliffs, *Level 2* (3–4) clear explanation of a process of coastal erosion using the correct terminology, e.g. sea water slowly dissolves chalk and limestone by the process of corrosion, *Level 3* (5–6) detailed explanation, a range of different types of coastal erosion are explained, e.g. waves smash into cliffs trapping air in cracks, air is compressed, increasing the pressure, forcing the rock to blow apart

COASTAL LANDFORMS

Section A
1 (c)
2 (a)
3 (d)
4 (b)
5 (a)

Section B
1 (e); (d); (a); (b); (c)
2 (a) Base of a cliff
   (b) Limestone
   (c) Sandstone

Section C
1 (a) A = Cave
       B = Arch
       C = Stump
       D = Stack
   (b) e.g. Old Harry, Dorset
   (c) *Level 1* (1–2) basic explanation, e.g. formed by erosion, *Level 2* (3–4) clear explanation, uses correct terms to explain how the stack is formed by erosion and suggests why the arch collapses, *Level 3* (5–6) detailed answer which explains in a logical sequence the formation of a stack from its beginnings as a crack in the cliff, using the correct terminology, explains how weathering contributes to the arch collapsing
2 (a) Headland = a point of higher land projecting into the sea (1), Bay = a curved break in the coastline (1)
   (b) Headlands and bays form in areas of alternating rock types (1), softer rock is eroded more quickly forming bays (1), harder rock is eroded more slowly forming headlands (1). Bays may also form along fault lines in coastal rocks (1)

COASTAL MANAGEMENT

Section A
1 (c)
2 (d)
3 (a)
4 (c)
5 (c)

Section B
1 (a) Beach nourishment
   (b) Groynes
   (c) Rock armour
   (d) Sea wall
   (e) Gabions
   (f) Cliff stabilisation
2 Hard engineering: Advantages = effective (1), benefits economy (1), disadvantages = expensive (1), may affect other areas (1)
   Soft engineering: Advantages = low cost (1), long term (1), disadvantages = loss of land/homes, (1) people upset (1)

Section C
1 (a) *Level 1* (1–2) explanation about waves undercutting base of cliffs or about cliffs collapsing through mass movement due to saturation with rain water, *Level 2* (3–4) explanation including both coastal erosion and mass movement processes
   (b) Injury (1), financial loss (1), psychological damage (1)
   (c) Land is of low economic value (1), buildings worth less than the cost of defences (1), lack of money to spend on defences (1), coastal erosion to severe to prevent (1)
   (d) *Level 1* (1–2) no example, focuses on problems rather than management, e.g. litter dropped by tourists, *Level 2* (3–4) named example, focuses on management of problems, e.g. litter bins are provided on beaches and are emptied regularly, *Level 3* (5–6) named example, focusing on management of a realistic range of different problems, e.g. litter, seasonal unemployment, damage to environment

GLACIATION

Section A
1 (c)
2 (b)
3 (a)
4 (d)
5 (c)

Section B
1 (a) Ablation
   (b) Accumulation
   (c) Deformation
   (d) Slippage
   (e) Plucking.
2 (b); (d); (e); (c); (a)

Section C
1 (a) Farming = valley floor suitable for dairy farming and some arable farming (1), valley sides suitable for pastoral farming such as sheep or goats (1) Communications = deep straight valleys provide routeways for road and rail (1), cable cars may link areas at higher altitudes (1) Tourism = skiing in winter (1), hiking in summer (1)
   (b) Hanging valleys may be dammed (1), relief rainfall/snow ensures supply of water (1)
   (c) Lack of flat land (1), extreme climate (1), poor communications (1), lack of job opportunities (1)
   (d) *Level 1* (1–2) no named example, problems caused by tourists simply described, e.g. environmental damage, *Level 2* (3–4) named example, problems described in more detail, e.g. Alps, deforestation to provide ski runs is causing soil erosion on valley sides

GLACIAL LANDFORMS

Section A
1 (b)
2 (c)
3 (d)
4 (a)
5 (b)

Section B
1 (a) Material deposited by a glacier (1), contains everything from clay to boulders (1), called glacial till (1)
   (b) A = Recessional
       B = Medial
       C = Terminal
       D = Lateral
   (c) A (recessional) – material deposited as the glacier retreated up the valley at the end of a glacial period (1), B (medial) – formed from two lateral moraines when two glaciers join together (1), C (terminal) – material deposited at the snout of the glacier as it melts (1), D (lateral) – material transported along the side of a glacier, accumulates due to freeze–thaw weathering (1)

Section C
1 (a) A = Pyramidal peak
       B = Arête
       C = Corrie
       D = Crevasse
   (b) e.g. Matterhorn
   (c) *Level 1* (1–2) basic explanation, e.g. formed by freeze–thaw weathering, *Level 2* (3–4) clear explanation, e.g. formed as three or more corries are weathered and eroded backwards into the mountain top, *Level 3* (5–6) detailed explanation as *Level 2*, but fully explains formation of corries through freeze–thaw, plucking and abrasion.
2 (a) Long, narrow hill (1), egg-shaped hill (1), formed from glacial till (1)
   (b) Material is deposited underneath glacier (1), towards the snout of the glacier (1), glacier continues moving forwards (1), shaping material into egg shape (1)

WEATHER

Section A
1 (b)
2 (d)
3 (c)
4 (d)
5 (c)

Section B
1 (a) Thermometer
   (b) Barometer
   (c) Anemometer
   (d) Wet and dry bulb thermometer

(e) Rain gauge

2 (b); (d); (c); (e); (a)

Section C

1 (a) A = Centre of depression
   B = Cold front
   C = Warm front
   D = Clear sky
   (b) Anti-clockwise
2 (a) Clouds thicken (1), it rains (1), temperature rises (1), then falls again (1), air pressure falls (1), then rises again (1), clouds break (1), wind direction changes (1)
   (b) *Level 1* (1–2) basic explanation, e.g. low pressure causes rainfall, *Level 2* (3–4) clear explanation, e.g. warm air meets cold air, warm air rises over cold air, cools, condenses and it rains, *Level 3* (5) detailed explanation as *Level 2*, but adds detail about warm and cold fronts

CLIMATE

Section A

1 (b)   4 (d)
2 (c)   5 (b)
3 (a)

Section B

1 (a) True
   (b) False
   (c) True
   (d) False
   (e) True
2 (a) Tropical grassland
   (b) Desert
   (c) Temperate maritime
   (d) Tropical
   (e) Mediterranean

Section C

1 (a) Cornwall/south-west England (1), southern Ireland (1)
   (b) East Scotland (1), north-east England (1), the Wash (1)
   (c) Temperatures decrease with distance from the equator (1), areas in the west are warmed by the North Atlantic Drift (warm ocean current) (1)
2 (a) Fort William
   (b) London
   (c) Wettest in west (1), driest in east (1)
   (d) Prevailing winds from south-west pick up moisture from Atlantic (1), wettest in west due to relief rainfall (1), driest in east due to 'rain shadow' effect (1)

WEATHER AND PEOPLE

Section A

1 (a)   4 (d)
2 (b)   5 (a)
3 (c)

Section B

1 (a) A long continuous period of dry weather

(b) e.g. Sahel, North Africa
(c) A third
(d) Using too much water (1), deforestation reducing evapo-transpiration (1), pollution causing global climate change (1)

2 (b); (a); (c); (e); (d)

Section C

1 (a) Began in Atlantic Ocean (1), moved north-west (1), then headed south-west (1), over Honduras (1), Guatemala (1), and Mexico (1), then headed back north-east (1), crossing Mexico again (1)
   (b) Honduras: 14,000 dead (1), Nicaragua: 3,500 dead (1), 725,000 homeless (1), 60% no electricity (1), El Salvador: 360 dead (1), 50,000 homeless (1), Guatemala: 440 dead (1), Belize: thousands evacuated (1), Mexico: 6 dead (1), thousands evacuated (1)
   (c) High winds (1) caused buildings to collapse (1), heavy rainfall caused flooding (1) and landslides (1), at the coast storm surges caused flooding (1)
   (d) *Level 1* (1–2) basic explanation, e.g. intense low pressure caused high winds, *Level 2* (3–4) clear explanation, e.g. sea temperature over 27°C, air rises causing low air pressure, drawing in winds from the side, and releases heavy rainfall, *Level 3* (5–6) detailed explanation as *Level 2*, but adds that air rises, cools and condenses, latent heat is released adding power to the hurricane, may explain why eye is 'calm'

POPULATION

Section A

1 (a)   4 (d)
2 (b)   5 (c)
3 (a)

Section B

1 (a) UK = 244.8, France = 108.2, Australia = 2.6, USA = 31.5, China = 137.2
   (b) UK
2 (a) Number of births per 1,000 people per year
   (b) Number of deaths per 1,000 people per year
   (c) Increase in population when birth rate exceeds death rate

Section C

1 (a) Mainly northern hemisphere (1), east and west USA (1), western Europe (1), India (1), south-east Asia (1)
   (b) Fairly evenly distributed (1), Canada (1), South America (1), north Africa (1), north

---

Russia (1), Asia (1), Australia (1)
   (c) High population density = flat land (1), temperate climate (1), fertile soil (1), good resources (1), jobs (1), low population density = mountainous land (1), harsh climate (1), poor soil (1), lack of resources (1), few jobs (1)
   (d) Any major city, e.g. London
   (e) e.g. flat land – easy for building (1), good communications such as roads and railways (1), plenty of jobs (1), people live in high-rise flats (1)
   (f) Census (1), questionnaire issued by governments (1), usually every 10 years (1), information about age, sex, ethnic group, etc. (1)

CHANGING POPULATIONS

Section A

1 (b)   4 (a)
2 (d)   5 (a)
3 (d)

Section B

1 (a) Stage 4
   (b) Stage 1
   (c) Stage 5
   (d) Stage 2
   (e) Stage 3

Section C

1 (a) Percentage of people in different age groups (1), percentage of males and females (1), life expectancy (1)
   (b) Wide base (1), steep concave sides (1), narrow peak (1)
   (c) High birth rate (1), large percentage of children (1), high infant mortality rate (1), high death rate (1), relatively short life expectancy (1)
   (d) Narrowing base (1), vertical sides (1), lower percentage of middle aged (1), relatively wide peak (1)
   (e) Low birth rate (1), low percentage of children (1), low infant mortality rate (1), low death rate (1), low birth rate following Second World War (1), long life expectancy (1)

MIGRATION

Section A

1 (a)   4 (b)
2 (b)   5 (c)
3 (b)

Section B

1 (a) e.g. moving from London to Oxfordshire for a new job
   (b) e.g. Mexican migrating to the USA
   (c) e.g. English person spending a year teaching in Uganda
   (d) e.g. Vietnamese person migrating to Australia

(e) e.g. Hutu fleeing Rwanda during civil war

2 (a) Push
   (b) Push
   (c) Pull
   (d) Push
   (e) Pull

Section C

1 (a) A person forced to leave their home country because of war, persecution or natural disasters
   (b) 13 million
   (c) Most are in Africa (1) or Asia (1), data included in answer (1), a country named in answer (1)
   (d) *Level 1* (1–2) basic suggestions, e.g. war, poverty, *Level 2* (3–4) detailed suggestions which link specific reasons or events, e.g. a high number of refugees originate from sub-Saharan Africa due to economic problems, war and drought
   (e) *Level 1* (1–2) basic description of causes or consequences, no named example, *Level 2* (3–4) clear description of causes and consequences, with a named example, *Level 3* (5) detailed description of causes and consequences classified in some way, e.g. push and pull factors, long-term and short-term effects, with a named example

SETTLEMENT

Section A

1 (c)   4 (b)
2 (d)   5 (c)
3 (d)

Section B

1 (a) Rock
   (b) Water
   (c) Soil
   (d) Wood
   (e) River
2 (a) 1
   (b) 5
   (c) 3
   (d) 4
   (e) 2

Section C

1 (a) A = Dispersed
   B = Nucleated
   C = Planned
   D = Linear
2 (a) The area served by a settlement (catchment are a)
   (b) Largest of the four shown (1), covers about half the city (1), extends to the east and south of the city boundary (1)
   (c) People are prepared to travel furthest to visit a hypermarket (1) because it has a greater range of products (1) and competitive prices (1). The suburban shopping centre

limits the hypermarket's sphere of influence to the west (1)

(d) There are many corner shops (1), therefore it is not necessary to travel far to visit one (1). Corner shops have a limited range of products (1) and prices are more expensive than larger stores (1)

SETTLEMENT IN MEDCS

Section A
1	(c)	4	(b)
2	(a)	5	(b)
3	(d)		

Section B
1 (a) A = Central Business District (CBD)
B = Transition zone
C = Low-cost housing
D = Medium-cost housing
E = High-cost housing
(b) CBD is in the centre as it is the most accessible place (1), housing cost may increase towards outskirts as houses become larger (1)

Section C
1 (a) People are living longer (1), more marriages are ending in divorce (1), people want to live in the countryside (1)
(b) Demand is concentrated in the south-east (1), particularly London (1) and Hampshire (1), in the north demand is focused around Manchester (1). Award maximum 2 marks for including data
(c) Area is more popular to live in (1), concentration of industry (1), attracts workers (1), younger population (1), close to major cities (1)
(d) Attractive to purchasers (1), land is easy to build on (1), as does not need to be cleaned up first (1)
(e) To protect the countryside from development (1), to help regenerate urban areas (1)

SETTLEMENT IN LEDCS

Section A
1	(c)	4	(c)
2	(d)	5	(b)
3	(a)		

Section B
1 (a) A = Central Business District (CBD)
B = Medium-cost housing
C = Low-cost housing
D = Shanty towns,
E = High-cost hosing or industry
(b) Shanty towns are not shown on MEDC model (1), housing quality in LEDC decreases towards the outskirts (1)

Section C
1 (a) Environment = low quality (1), rubbish (1), dry (1), dusty (1), trees (1), housing = low quality (1), shacks (1), crowded (1), wood (1), plastic (1), corrugated metal (1)
(b) Employment = high unemployment (1), lack of formal jobs (1), housing = shortage of housing (1), lack of amenities (1), services = lack of services (1), e.g. schools and health centres (1)
(c) *Level 1* (1–2) basic description of urban improvements, no named example or may be MEDC, *Level 2* (3–4) clear description of how problems are being tackled in a named LEDC city, *Level 3* (5) detailed and realistic description of how a named LEDC city is tackling problems, possibly classified, e.g. unemployment, transport, housing or services

AGRICULTURE

Section A
1	(b)	4	(d)
2	(b)	5	(b)
3	(c)		

Section B
1 (a) Western England
(b) East England
(c) South-east England
(d) Upland Wales
2 (a) Pastoral
(b) Nomadic
(c) Arable
(d) Mixed
(e) Intensive
(f) Subsistence

Section C
1 (a) Mixture of arable crops (1), largest land use is grass (1), followed by willow biomass (1), variety of woodland (1), oilseed rape (1), wheat (1), barley (1), set-aside (1)
(b) Arable (1), commercial (1), sedentary (1)
(c) Inputs = seeds (1), labour (1), fertiliser (1), processes = ploughing (1), planting (1), harvesting (1), outputs = crops (1), waste materials (1)
(d) Rainfall (1), temperature (1), growing season (1), altitude (1), aspect (1), relief (1), soil (1)
(e) Labour (1), market (1), accessibility (1), subsidies (1), quotas (1), attitudes (1)

AGRICULTURAL CHANGE

Section A
1	(d)	4	(b)
2	(c)	5	(a)
3	(b)		

Section B
1 (a) Increased
(b) Without
(c) Natural
(d) Removed
(e) Decrease
2 (a) True
(b) False
(c) True
(d) False
(e) False

Section C
1 (a) Correctly plotted bar graph (2 × 1)
(b) Developed countries
(c) Africa
(d) Asia
(e) Introduction of capital intensive farming methods (1), high-yield variety crops (1), fertilisers (1), herbicides (1), pesticides (1), irrigation (1), mechanisation (1)
(f) *Level 1* (1–2) basic answer, benefits or problems, no named example, *Level 2* (3–4) clear answer, benefits and problems but unbalanced, named example, *Level 3* (5–6) detailed answer, benefits and problems balanced, named example, e.g. India, yields of rice increased by three times, now possible to grow two crops a year, but mechanisation increased rural unemployment, monoculture carries greater risk of disease

INDUSTRY

Section A
1	(b)	4	(c)
2	(b)	5	(c)
3	(b)		

Section B
1 (b); (a); (d); (c); (e)
2 (a) Market
(b) Transport
(c) Labour
(d) Capital
(e) Environment

Section C
1 (a) Percentage of workers involved in primary, secondary and tertiary industry in an area
(b) A = primary 60%, secondary 10%, tertiary 30%, B = primary 40%, secondary 40 %, tertiary 20%, C = primary 8%, secondary 3%, tertiary 62%
(c) C
2 (a) Primary decreased (1), secondary decreased (1), tertiary increased (1), quaternary increased (1)
(b) Primary decreased due to mechanisation (1), secondary decreased due to closure of factories (1) as a result of cheaper imports (1), tertiary increased due to growth of industries such

as leisure (1), retail (1), finance (1), quaternary increased due to research and development into new technology (1) such as bio-technology (1)

INDUSTRY IN MEDCS

Section A
1	(b)	4	(d)
2	(c)	5	(a)
3	(c)		

Section B
1 (a) Business park
(b) Industrial estate
(c) Retail park
(d) Science park
2 (a) Yorkshire
(b) Lancashire
(c) Nottinghamshire
(d) South Wales
3 (a) Able to locate anywhere
(b) Site not previously built on

Section C
1 (a) Correctly plotted bar graph (2 × 1)
(b) Japan
(c) United States
(d) Decrease in number of workers
(e) (2 × 1) South Wales (1), Midlands (1), north-east England (1), central Scotland (1), (2 x 1) close to raw materials (1), iron ore (1), coal (1), limestone (1)
(f) *Level 1* (1–2) basic description of decline of steel industry, *Level 2* (3–4) clear explanation of either competition from abroad or loss of overseas markets, *Level 3* (5–6) detailed explanation of both competition and loss of markets

INDUSTRY IN LEDCS

Section A
1	(a)	4	(c)
2	(a)	5	(a)
3	(d)		

Section B
1 (a) Formal
(b) Informal
(c) Formal
(d) Formal
(e) Informal
(f) Informal
2 (a) 1
(b) 2
(c) 3
(d) 4

Section C
1 (a) 193 million
(b) Gross Domestic Product
(c) China
(d) Malaysia
(e) 7.34%
(f) Named country, e.g. Thailand (1), cheap loans and subsidies given (1) to establish new industries (1), imports restricted (1) to protect new industries (1),

currencies devalued (1) to make exports cheaper (1), education prioritised (1) to attract high-tech companies (1)

(g) *Level 1* (1–2) basic ideas, successes or problems, no named example, *Level 2* (3–4) clear description of successes or problems, but unbalanced, a named example, *Level 3* (5–6) detailed description, well balanced between successes and problems of a named example, e.g. South Korea, has developed successful high-tech industries which have expanded globally, wages and living standards of Koreans have risen, but global recession has resulted in some companies going bankrupt, high levels of debt have caused economic problems, wages have risen causing transnational companies to relocate to cheaper countries

TOURISM

Section A
1 (c)   4 (a)
2 (d)   5 (a)
3 (b)

Section B
1 (a) Scenery
   (b) Climate
   (c) Ecology
   (d) Culture
2 (a) Social = local culture and traditions preserved, environmental = environment is protected, economic = employment and incomes increase
   (b) Social = local culture is lost, environmental = ecosystems are damaged, economic = traditional jobs replaced by seasonal/ unreliable work

Section C
1 (a) Correctly plotted bar graph (3 × 1)
   (b) Increase (1), data, e.g. of 180 million tourist arrivals (1)
   (c) Increases in paid holiday (1), wages (1), car ownership (1) and life expectancy (1), decreases in working week (1) and air fares (1), changes in attitude and lifestyle (1)
   (d) *Level 1* (1–2) basic description of increase in foreign holidays, *Level 2* (3–4) clear description of transition from UK based holidays to foreign travel as a result of package holidays, *Level 3* (5–6) detailed description of transition from UK seaside holidays to Mediterranean package holidays to long-haul destinations such as the

USA, Asia and Africa. Describes how resorts declined in popularity

TOURISM CASE STUDIES

Section A
1 (b)   4 (d)
2 (d)   5 (c)
3 (b)

Section B
1 (a) False
   (b) False
   (c) True
   (d) True
   (e) False
2 A = Yorkshire Dales
   B = Norfolk Broads
   C = Dartmoor
   D = Brecon Beacons
   E = Snowdonia

Section C
1 (a) Tourism which encourages smaller groups of tourists (1) and tries to limit impacts on the environment (1)
   (b) South-east (1) Peru (1)
   (c) Wildlife (1) such as macaws, otters and eagles (1), opportunity to stay with local people – Ese'eja Indians (1) and to participate in natural and cultural education programmes (1)
   (d) *Level 1* (1–2) basic answer, sustainability not understood, but comments on environmental protection, e.g. wildlife is protected, *Level 2* (3–4) clear answer, demonstrates some understanding of sustainability, e.g. money from tourism is used to protect wildlife, *Level 3* (5–6) detailed answer, illustrates full understanding of sustainability – conserving the environment for future generations – e.g. local community earns money from tourism and therefore it is in their interests to preserve the rainforest rather than exploit it for short-term gains

RESOURCES

Section A
1 (c)   4 (a)
2 (a)   5 (b)
3 (c)

Section B
1 (a) Renewable
   (b) Non-renewable
   (c) Renewable
   (d) Non-reewable
   (e) Renewable
   (f) Non-renewable
2 Rubber = synthetic rubber, cotton = nylon, petrol = liquid petroleum gas, tin cans = aluminium

Section C
1 (a) Turning waste into new products (1), using things more than once (1)
   (b) Glass (1), paper (1), car batteries (1), plastic (1), organic waste (1), steel (1), textiles (1), aluminium (1)
   (c) Conserves resources (1), saves energy (1), reduces pollution (1), reduces waste (1)
   (d) Noise (1), mess (1), unsightly (1), danger (1)
   (e) Landfill (1) 83% (1), incineration (1) 9% (1)

ENERGY

Section A
1 (d)   4 (d)
2 (b)   5 (c)
3 (b)

Section B
1 (a) 200
   (b) 45
   (c) 300
   (d) 300
   (e) 400
2 (a) Finite
   (b) 1,000
   (c) Upland
   (d) Impermeable
   (e) Secondary

Section C
1 (a) Uneven (1), more used by MEDCs (1), most used by the USA (1), least used in Africa (1), data in answer (2 × 1)
   (b) Population growth (1), will increase demand by 50% in 20 years (1), economic development (1) will result in more appliances such as fridges which use energy (1), in MEDCs energy consumption may decrease (1) due to more energy-efficient appliances (1)
   (c) *Level 1* (1–2) basic, not necessarily specific to one type of renewable energy, *Level 2* (3) clear example which describes how the energy resource is turned into electricity
   (d) *Level 1* (1–2) basic suggestions, may not be balanced between advantages and disadvantages, *Level 2* (3–4) clear and realistic suggestions, balanced between advantages and disadvantages

DEVELOPMENT

Section A
1 (b)   4 (b)
2 (d)   5 (b)
3 (a)

Section B
1 (a) Prestige
   (b) Appropriate technology
   (c) Appropriate technology

   (d) Prestige
   (e) Prestige
   (f) Appropriate technology
2 (a) 4
   (b) 1
   (c) 3
   (d) 2

Section C
1 (a) The use of resources and technology to increase wealthand improve standards of living
   (b) Data correctly plotted (2 × 1)
   (c) Best fit line accurately drawn
   (d) The greater the GNP per capita, the lower the population per doctor (2), this is a negative relationship (correlation) (1)
   (e) *Level 1* (1–2) basic suggestions, e.g. richer countries have more doctors, *Level 2* (3–4) detailed suggestions, e.g. countries with a higher GNP per capita are able to spend more on healthcare per person, richer countries tend to have lower populations, richer countries do not have to make such large national debt repayments
   (f) Value of money varies between countries (1), a dollar can buy much more in India than in America (1), GNP cannot measure human factors (1) such as life expectancy (1) or education (1)

TRADE AND AID

Section A
1 (b)   4 (a)
2 (c)   5 (d)
3 (a)

Section B
1 (a) NGO aid
   (b) Emergency aid
   (c) Multilateral aid
   (d) Long–term aid
   (e) Bilateral aid
2 (a) True
   (b) True
   (c) False
   (d) False
   (e) True

Section C
1 (a) The exchange of goods (1) and/or services (1)
   (b) Northern hemisphere (1), MEDCs (1), America (1), Europe (1), NICs (1), Asia (1)
   (c) Countries are either MEDCs or NICs (1), who have well developed manufacturing industries (1), based either on technology and mechanisation (1) or on cheap labour (1)
   (d) Relatively evenly distributed (1), South America (1),

Africa (1), South-east Asia (1), northern Europe (1)

(e) Countries are LEDCs (1) who not have well developed manufacturing industries (1) or countries are rich in raw materials (1) such as timber or metal ores (1)

(f) *Level 1* (1–2) basic comments on advantages or disadvantages, *Level 2* (3–4) clear comments on advantages and disadvantages, *Level 3* (5) detailed comments on advantages and disadvantages from perspective of both MEDCs and LEDCs, e.g. pattern of trade is more advantageous for MEDCs, price of manufactured goods has increased steadily, competition between LEDCs means MEDCs buy goods for lowest possible price, LEDCs cannot afford to buy all manufactured goods needed, exploitation of raw materials in LEDCs is damaging the environment

ECOSYSTEMS

Section A
1 (a) 4 (b)
2 (d) 5 (a)
3 (c)

Section B
1 A = Temperate grassland
  B = Coniferous forest
  C = Tundra
  D = Deciduous woodland
  E = Mediterranean
  F = Desert
  G = Tropical grassland
  H = Tropical rainforest
2 Sunlight (1), temperature (1), rainfall (1)

Section C
1 (a) Sun
  (b) Energy passes through an ecosystem in a food chain as one organism eats another (1), a food web shows how food chains are interconnected (1)
  (c) Worm (1), snail (1), mouse (1), rabbit (1)
  (d) Level 3
  (e) *Level 1* (1–2) basic answer, e.g. one fox needs to eat lots of mice to survive, *Level 2* (3–4) detailed answer, e.g. only a small percentage of energy is transferred from one trophic level to the next, as much is lost through living processes such as respiration
  (f) *Level 1* (1–2) basic, no named example, comments on energy flow or nutrient cycle, *Level 2* (3–4) clear, named example, comments on energy flows and nutrient cycles but not

balanced, *Level 3* (5) detailed, named example, balanced comments on energy flows and nutrient cycles, e.g. Australian tropical grassland, introduction of rabbits altered energy flows, rabbits ate grass, decreasing numbers of indigenous wildlife on same trophic level, wheat farmers added nutrients to the ecosystem in the form of artificial fertilisers, nutrients are removed from system when wheat is harvested

GLOBAL ENVIRONMENTS

Section A
1 (b) 4 (a)
2 (d) 5 (c)
3 (a)

Section B
1 (a) 5°
  (b) Red clay
  (c) High
  (d) Daily
  (e) Deforestation
2 A = Litter
  B = Humus
  C = Leaching,
  D = Weathering
  E = Bedrock

Section C
1 (a) 25° north and south of the equator (1), in central parts of continents (1), central Africa (1), South America (1), Northern Australia (1)
  (b) Grassland (1), short trees (1), with wide-spreading branches (1)
  (c) High temperatures (1) throughout year (1), average 35°C (1), wet and dry seasons (1)
  (d) *Level 1* (1–2) basic, small number of adaptations described, *Level 2* (3–4) clear, number of adaptations described and explained, *Level 3* (5–6) detailed, number of adaptations to different aspects of the climate are described and explained, e.g. small waxy leaves reduced water loss during wet season and leaves are dropped to prevent water loss during dry season, grass roots spread outwards to collect water during wet seasons and die back to the roots during the dry season

GLOBAL WARMING

Section A
1 (c) 4 (c)
2 (a) 5 (b)
3 (a)

Section B
1 (a) True

(b) True
(c) True
(d) True
(e) True
2 (a) 3°C
  (b) 5°C
  (c) 7°C
  (d) 4°C
  (e) 2°C

Section C
1 (a) Greenhouse effect is the way the Earth's atmosphere traps heat from the sun (1), global warming is an increase in the average temperature of the Earth (1)
  (b) Earth's average temperature has increased (1) by 0.6°C in the past 100 years (1), glaciers and ice sheets are melting (1), extreme weather events have increased (1), ecosystems are changing (1)
  (c) *Level 1* (1–2) descriptive answer, e.g. the Americans contribute to global warming by driving large cars, *Level 2* (3–4) explanatory answer, e.g. the Americans are the largest emitters of greenhouse gases but they refuse to reduce their emissions of CO_2 as they believe it will reduce living standards
  (d) Fossil fuels = fossil fuels are burned to provide energy (1), releasing CO_2 into the atmosphere (1), Deforestation = trees convert CO_2 into oxygen, reducing global warming (1), when they have been cut down trees are often burned releasing CO_2 into the atmosphere (1), Methane = methane gas is added to the atmosphere by bacteria in rice fields (1), rotting waste in rubbish dumps (1) and by flatulent cattle (1)

ACID RAIN

Section A
1 (a) 4 (d)
2 (b) 5 (c)
3 (d)

Section B
1 (a) Nutrients are leached from the soil, making it infertile
  (b) Trees turn yellow, drop their leaves and die
  (c) Lakes become acidic and wildlife may die
  (d) Water supplies may become contaminated
  (e) Limestone and marble buildings are attacked by chemical weathering
2 (a) False
  (b) True
  (c) True
  (d) False
  (e) True

Section C
1 (a) Rainwater that has become

acidic (1) due to pollution (1)
  (b) Uneven distribution (1), lowest in the west (1), highest in the north-east (1), data (2 × 1)
  (c) Air pollution (1) from burning fossil fuels (1), nitrogen oxide (1), sulphur dioxide (1), combines with rainfall (1)
  (d) Concentration of industry in the north-east (1), prevailing wind direction (1)
  (e) Acid rain may cross borders (1), travelling up to 2,000km (1), e.g. acid rain caused by the UK affects Norway and Sweden (1), this results in conflict between the countries (1)

USE AND ABUSE OF THE ENVIRONMENT – WATER

Section A
1 (c) 4 (c)
2 (d) 5 (c)
3 (c)

Section B
1 (a) Half a mark per accurately plotted dot
  (b) Best fit line accurately drawn
  (c) As population increases, the amount of water used also increases (1), this is a positive relationship (1)

Section C
1 (a) Northern hemisphere (1), North America (1), North Africa (1), Europe (1), China (1)
  (b) North Africa (1), Middle East (1), Asia (1), South Africa (1)
  (c) *Level 1* (1–2) basic ideas, e.g. lack of rainfall, *Level 2* (3–4) clear ideas relating to population growth, development or climate change, e.g. rapid global population growth in these areas will put increasing pressure on limited supplies, *Level 3* (5–6) detailed ideas relating to at least two of the following: population growth, development or climate change, e.g. large increase in global population will use up more resources, including water. Pollution created by extra people may contribute to global warming, reducing rainfall in some areas
  (d) Transfer water from areas of surplus to areas of deficit (1), build more reservoirs (1), build desalination plants (1), prevent water pollution (1), repaire leaking supply pipes (1), save water, e.g. use waste water from baths to flush toilets (1)

USE AND ABUSE OF THE ENVIRONMENT – LAND

Section A
1 (c)
2 (c)
3 (d)
4 (c)
5 (a)

Section B
1 (a) Short term
   (b) Long term
   (c) Long term
   (d) Short term
   (e) Short term
   (f) Long term
2 (a) Lines of stones are placed along contours to slow surface run-off and limit soil erosion
   (b) Land is ploughed parallel to contours to limit soil erosion
   (c) Trees act as wind breaks to limit wind erosion
   (d) Drought-resistant plants may be used to stabilise sand dunes

Section C
1 (a) The spread of desert-like conditions into dry grassland areas
   (b) Unevenly distributed (1), but present in every continent (1), zones above and below the equator (1), next to existing deserts (1), tend to be on western sides of continents (1)
   (c) Climate change = many years of drought (1), average rainfall is decreasing (1), possible link to global climate change (1), Population growth = rapid global population growth (1), more food is needed (1), more fragile areas are being farmed (1), Overgrazing = increase in numbers of cattle and goats (1), has removed vegetation leaving soil exposed to erosion (1), Irrigation = pumping up water from underground has lowered water table (1), tree and plant roots cannot longer get water and die (1), Deforestation = trees cut down for fuel wood (1), soil no longer held together and washed away (1)

MAP SKILLS

Section A
1 (b)
2 (a)
3 (c)
4 (c)
5 (a)

Section B
1 (a) Spit
   (b)

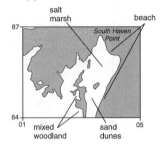

Section C
1 99 square kilometres
2 South-east (1), east south-east (1)
3 3–4 kilometres
4 21 metres
5 Roman road
6 0094 = newer housing (1), winding streets (1), semi-detached (1), 0492 = older housing (1), straight streets (1), terraced (1)
7 North = residential (1), transport (1), industry (1), south = woodland (1), farmland (1), marshland (1)
8 Oil wells
9 Wide river estuary (1), small tributary rivers have wide channels (1), original channels can be seen between mudflats (1)
10 4_ hours
11 Ferry only runs in summer
12 Four examples, or two examples with grid references, e.g. aquarium (1), at 010904 (1), tourist information office (1), at 009903 (1)

LETTS EDUCATIONAL
The Chiswick Centre
414 Chiswick High Road
London W4 5TF
Tel: 020 8996 3333
Fax: 020 8742 8390
Email: mail@lettsed.co.uk
Website: www.letts-education.com

C **These are GCSE-style questions. Answer all parts of the questions.**

1 Study the photograph below, which shows a typical shanty town.

(a) Describe the buildings and the environment shown in the photograph.

....

....

....

.... (4 marks)

(b) Describe the problems of shanty towns under the following headings.

Employment ....

.... (2 marks)

Housing ....

.... (2 marks)

Services ....

.... (2 marks)

(c) With reference to an example you have studied, explain how a city in an LEDC is tackling problems caused by rapid urban growth.

....

....

....

....

....

(5 marks)

Score   /15

How well did you do?

0–7 correct   Try again
8–14 correct   Getting there
15–20 correct   Good work
21–27 correct   Excellent!

TOTAL SCORE   /27

For more on this topic
see pages 52–53 of your Success Guide

AGRICULTURE

A Choose just one answer, a, b, c or d.

1 How much rainfall do most crops need each year?
(a) 250–300 mm
(b) 300–350 mm
(c) 350–400 mm
(d) 400–450 mm   (1 mark)

2 What is the minimum temperature crops need to be able to grow?
(a) 5°C   (b) 6°C
(c) 7°C   (d) 8°C   (1 mark)

3 What is the length of the growing season for wheat?
(a) 70 days   (b) 80 days
(c) 90 days   (d) 100 days   (1 mark)

4 Which of the following is not a human factor which influences farming?
(a) Labour
(b) Market
(c) Access
(d) Relief   (1 mark)

5 What is a quota?
(a) A subsidy
(b) A limit on production
(c) The price of a crop
(d) A demand for produce   (1 mark)

Score   /5

B Answer all parts of all questions.

1 Match the following types of farming with the most appropriate location.

(a) Dairy farming ....

(b) Arable farming ....

(c) Market gardening ....

(d) Sheep farming ....

| Western England |
| Upland Wales |
| Eastern England |
| South-east England |

(4 marks)

2 Match the descriptions below with the most appropriate classification.

(a) Sheep farming in Wales ....

(b) Maasai cattle herders in Kenya ....

(c) Rice farming in Japan ....

(d) Wheat and cattle farming in Brazil ....

(e) Tomato growing in Spain ....

(f) Crofting in Scotland ....

| pastoral |
| arable |
| nomadic |
| subsistence |
| intensive |
| mixed |

(6 marks)
Score   /10

C These are GCSE-style questions. Answer all parts of the questions.

1 Study the map, which shows the land use at Roves Farm in 1999. Roves Farm is located 5 km east of Swindon, Wiltshire.

(a) Describe the land use at Roves Farm.

....

....

....

....

....

....

....

....

(4 marks)

Roves Farm: 1999 harvest

to Sevenhampton

Roves Farm

0   200 m

key
- lime trees in grass
- oilseed rape
- grass
- winter barley
- wild flower meadow
- wheat
- set-aside
- willow biomass
- ♣♣ broad-leaved woodland
- ⫿⫿⫿ wide-spread poplars

River Cole

railway
to Swindon   A420   to Shrivenham

(b) Based on the information provided, suggest how the farm may be classified.

....

.... (2 marks)

(c) For one of the crops grown on the farm, complete the systems diagram below.

Inputs	**Processes**	**Outputs**
	→	→		

(5 marks)

(d) How might physical factors influence what is grown on the farm?

....

.... (2 marks)

(e) How might human factors influence what is grown on the farm?

....

.... (2 marks)

Score   /15

How well did you do?

0–8 correct   Try again
9–15 correct   Getting there
16–23 correct   Good work
24–30 correct   Excellent!

TOTAL SCORE   /30

For more on this topic
see pages 54–55 of your Success Guide

AGRICULTURAL CHANGE

A

Choose just one answer, a, b, c or d.

1 Set-aside is a scheme that pays farmers to leave their fields fallow. Which description best describes set-aside?
(a) 5% of land left fallow for 20 years
(b) 5% of land left fallow for 5 years
(c) 20% of land left fallow for 20 years
(d) 20% of land left fallow for 5 years
(1 mark)

2 How much are farmers paid for each hectare of set-aside land each year?
(a) £100 (b) £200
(c) £300 (d) £400 (1 mark)

3 Which of the following is allowed on set-aside land?
(a) Wheat (b) Trees

(c) Barley (d) Maize (1 mark)

4 Who funds the set-aside scheme?
(a) The UK government
(b) The European Union
(c) The National Farmers Union
(d) The local authority (1 mark)

5 Which of the following is not a type of farm diversification on an arable farm?
(a) Growing oil seed rape
(b) Opening a tea shop
(c) Growing a willow maze
(d) Opening an animal farm park (1 mark)

Score /5

B

Answer all parts of all questions.

1 Cross out the incorrect words in the sentences below.

(a) Demand for organic produce has increased/decreased in the UK in recent years.

(b) Organic meat is produced by rearing animals with/without the use of chemicals.

(c) Organic crops are grown using natural/artificial fertilisers.

(d) Modern farming methods have added/removed over 350,000 km of hedgerows in the UK.

(e) Overuse of fertiliser leads to an increase/decrease in river wildlife. (5 marks)

2 Decide whether the statements below are true or false.

	True	False
(a) The Green Revolution has widened the gap between rich and poor farmers	☐	☐
(b) Leguminous crops remove nitrogen from the soil, decreasing fertility	☐	☐
(c) The Common Agricultural Policy (CAP) aims to protect farmers' incomes	☐	☐
(d) The CAP resulted in food shortages	☐	☐
(e) The CAP is very cost-effective	☐	☐

(5 marks)

Score /10

C **These are GCSE-style questions.**
Answer all parts of the questions.

1 The Green Revolution was
the introduction of high
technology farming
methods during the 1960s.
Study the graph, which
shows how cereal yields
have been affected by the
Green Revolution.

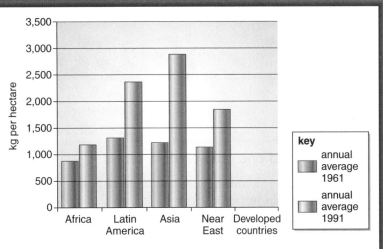

key
annual average 1961
annual average 1991

(a) Complete the graph using the data in this table.

Developed countries	
1961	1,700 kg/ha
1991	3,100 kg/ha

(2 marks)

(b) Which region produced the highest yield in 1991?

.... (1 mark)

(c) Which region had the smallest increase in yield between 1961 and 1991?

.... (1 mark)

(d) Which region has benefited most from the Green Revolution?

.... (1 mark)

(e) Describe the technological improvements which led to the Green Revolution.

....

....

....

.... (4 marks)

(f) With reference to an example you have studied, describe the benefits and
problems as a result of the Green Revolution.

....

....

....

....

....

.... (6 marks)

Score   /15

How well did you do?

0–8 correct   Try again
9–15 correct   Getting there
16–23 correct Good work
24–30 correct Excellent!

For more on this topic
see pages 56–57 of your Success Guide

INDUSTRY

Choose just one answer, a, b, c or d.

1 Which of the following is an example of a job in primary industry?
(a) Baker   (b) Farmer
(c) Electrician   (d) Beautician   (1 mark)

2 Which of the following is an example of a job in secondary industry?
(a) Miner
(b) Steel worker
(c) Policewoman
(d) Forester   (1 mark)

3 Which of the following is an example of a job in tertiary industry?
(a) Carpenter   (b) Teacher
(c) Builder   (d) Welder   (1 mark)

4 Which of the following is an example of a job in quaternary industry?
(a) Tree surgeon
(b) Garden landscaper
(c) Research scientist
(d) Film editor   (1 mark)

5 Which of the following is a process in an industrial system?
(a) Labour
(b) Energy
(c) Assembly
(d) Capital   (1 mark)

Score   /5

B **Answer all parts of all questions.**

1 Arrange the following statements in the correct order to explain the multiplier effect.

(a) Jobs are created. ☐

(b) Other industries are needed to provide components and services. ☐

(c) Local shops and leisure facilities benefit. ☐

(d) Workers have more money to spend. ☐

(e) The area becomes more popular to live in. ☐   (5 marks)

2 Match the descriptions below with the correct location factor.

(a) People who purchase goods or services ....   market

(b) Road, rail, sea and air networks ....   labour

(c) Employees with different skills ....   transport

(d) Money to invest in the industry ....   environment

(e) Leisure facilities ....   capital

(5 marks)

Score   /10

These are GCSE-style questions. Answer all parts of the questions.

1 Study the graph, which shows the occupational structures of three different countries, A, B and C.

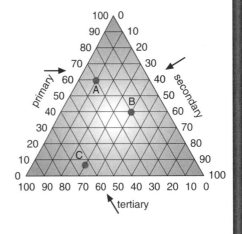

(a) What is meant by the term 'occupational structure'?

....

....

(1 mark)

(b) Calculate the occupational structures for the three countries.

....

....

....

.... (3 marks)

(c) Which country is the most developed?

.... (1 mark)

2 Study the pie charts below, which show how the UK's occupational structure has changed over the past 100 years.

1900

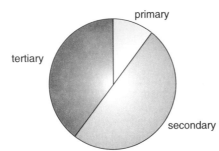

2000

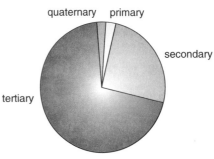

(a) Describe how the UK's employment structure has changed between 1900 and 2000.

....

....

.... (3 marks)

(b) Suggest why the UK's occupational structure has changed in this way.

....

....

....

.... (4 marks)

Score   /12

How well did you do?

0–7 correct   Try again
8–14 correct   Getting there
15–20 correct   Good work
21–27 correct   Excellent!

TOTAL SCORE   /27

**For more on this topic
see pages 58–59 of your Success Guide**

INDUSTRY IN MEDCS

A **Choose just one answer, a, b, c or d.**

1 Which of the following is the best example of light manufacturing?
(a) Mini car factory   (b) Doritos crisp factory
(c) Oil refinery   (d) Gap factory store
(1 mark)

2 Which of the following is the best example of a high technology industry?
(a) Oven chip factory
(b) British Gas call centre
(c) Nokia mobile phone factory
(d) McDonald's restaurant   (1 mark)

3 Which of the following is the best example of a retail industry?
(a) Coca Cola factory (b) Sony hi-fi factory
(c) Levi factory store   (d) Flour mill
(1 mark)

4 Which of the following is the best example of a leisure industry?
(a) Burger King restaurant
(b) Nike factory
(c) Direct Line Insurance call centre
(d) UCI cinema   (1 mark)

5 Which is the best example of an administrative industry?
(a) British Telecom call centre
(b) Dell computer factory
(c) Copper ore mine
(d) Taxi company   (1 mark)

Score   /5

B **Answer all parts of all questions.**

1 Match the descriptions of industries below with their most appropriate locations.

(a) A mixture of light manufacturing, offices and retail

(b) Light manufacturing industries

(c) A mixture of large shops and leisure facilities

(d) Hi-tech companies linked to a university

| industrial estate |
| business park |
| science park |
| retail park |

(4 marks)

2 Complete the following sentences about the original location of heavy industries using the words below.

(a) The wool industry developed in ....

(b) The cotton industry developed in ....

(c) The coal industry developed in ....

(d) The iron and steel industry developed in ....

| Nottinghamshire |
| South Wales |
| Yorkshire |
| Lancashire |

(4 marks)

3 Define the following terms.

(a) Footloose industry .... (1 mark)

(b) Greenfield site.. (1 mark)

Score   /10

C These are GCSE-style questions. Answer all parts of the questions.

1 Study the graph below, which shows changes in employment in the steel industry.

(a) Complete the graph using the data in the table below.

Japan	
1974	450,000
2000	190,000

(2 marks)

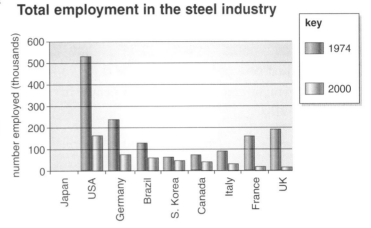

Total employment in the steel industry

key
1974
2000

number employed (thousands)

Japan, USA, Germany, Brazil, S. Korea, Canada, Italy, France, UK

(b) Which country employed the greatest number of people in the steel industry in 2000?

.... (1 mark)

(c) Which country had the greatest change in employment between 1974 and 2000?

.... (1 mark)

(d) What is the overall trend in employment in the steel industry in the countries shown?

.... (1 mark)

(e) Describe and explain the location of the iron and steel industry in the UK during the Industrial Revolution.

....

....

....

.... (4 marks)

(f) Explain why the steel industry has declined in the UK since the 1960s.

....

....

....

....

....

.... (6 marks)

Score   /15

How well did you do?

0–8 correct	Try again
9–15 correct	Getting there
16–23 correct	Good work
24–30 correct	Excellent!

TOTAL SCORE   /30

For more on this topic
see pages 60–61 of your Success Guide

INDUSTRY IN LEDCS

A

Choose just one answer, a, b, c or d.

1 In which employment sector do most people in LEDCs work?
(a) Primary   (b) Secondary
(c) Tertiary   (d) Quaternary   (1 mark)

2 Which of the following is not a problem for LEDCs seeking to industrialise?
(a) Cheap labour
(b) Unreliable electricity
(c) Limited capital investment
(d) Lack of local markets   (1 mark)

3 Which of the following is not a reason for transnational corporations (TNCs) to locate in LEDCs?
(a) Access to new markets
(b) Low labour costs
(c) Trade barriers can be avoided

(d) High taxes   (1 mark)

4 Which is an advantage brought by TNCs locating in LEDCs?
(a) TNCs may influence government policy
(b) Profit is transferred to MEDCs
(c) Employment is provided for local people
(d) Wages are low and working conditions poor   (1 mark)

5 Which is a disadvantage brought by TNCs locating in LEDCs?
(a) Many of the jobs are low skilled
(b) Taxes are paid to the government
(c) Technology is transferred to the LEDC
(d) Infrastructure and services may be improved   (1 mark)

Score   /5

B

Answer all parts of all questions.

1 Classify the jobs below into either the formal sector or the informal sector.

(a) Factory worker.   (b) Street food vendor.

(c) Telephone operator.   (d) Office worker.

(e) Shoe shiner.   (f) Magazine seller.   (6 marks)

Formal sector	Informal sector

2 Rank the four countries below in order of the amount earned by factory workers. The highest should be number 1.

(a) Italy   ☐

(b) USA   ☐

(c) China   ☐

(d) Bangladesh   ☐   (4 marks)

Score   /10

C **These are GCSE-style questions. Answer all parts of the questions.**

1 Study the table below, which contains data about five Newly Industrialising Countries (NICs) in Asia.

Country	Population (millions)	GDP (US$ billions)	GDP per capita (US$)	Economic growth forecast
China	1,280	715	592	9.0%
Indonesia	193	179	927	7.0%
Malaysia	20	88	4,397	7.5%
Philippines	70	74	1,054	5.5%
Thailand	60	167	2,789	7.7%

(a) What is the population of Indonesia?

.... (1 mark)

(b) What is meant by the abbreviation 'GDP'?

.... (1 mark)

(c) Which country has the highest GDP?

.... (1 mark)

(d) Which country earns the highest amount of money per person?

.... (1 mark)

(e) What is the average economic growth forecast for the five NICs?

.... (1 mark)

(f) With reference to a NIC you have studied, explain how the government achieved rapid industrial development.

....

....

.... (4 marks)

(g) Describe the successes and problems of economic growth experienced by the NIC you have studied.

....

....

....

.... (6 marks)

Score   /15

How well did you do?

0–8 correct   Try again
9–15 correct   Getting there
16–23 correct   Good work
24–30 correct   Excellent!

TOTAL SCORE   /30

For more on this topic see pages 62–63 of your Success Guide

59

TOURISM

A **Choose just one answer, a, b, c or d.**

1 Which of the following is the best description of tourism?
(a) A visit to a foreign country
(b) A visit for recreation
(c) A visit for enjoyment which includes an overnight stay
(d) A visit for work which includes an overnight stay (1 mark)

2 How many tourist visits occur globally each year?
(a) 420 million   (b) 495 million
(c) 560 million   (d) 635 million   (1 mark)

3 Approximately how many tourists visit the UK each year?
(a) 20 million   (b) 25 million
(c) 30 million   (d) 35 million   (1 mark)

4 How much is contributed to the UK economy by tourism each year?
(a) £14 billion   (b) £15 billion
(c) £16 billion   (d) £17 billion   (1 mark)

5 Which country is the most popular international tourist destination in the world?
(a) France   (b) Spain
(c) USA   (d) Italy   (1 mark)

Score   /5

B **Answer all parts of all questions.**

1 Match the following descriptions of holidays with the most important tourism factor.

(a) A walking holiday in Nepal

(b) A snowboarding holiday in the USA

(c) A safari in Kenya

(d) A weekend break in Barcelona

climate

scenery

ecology

culture

(4 marks)

2 Complete the table below to show how tourism can have positive and negative impacts.   (6 marks)

	a) Positive impacts	b) Negative impacts
Social		
Environmental		
Economic		

Score   /10

C **These are GCSE-style questions. Answer all parts of the questions.**

1 Study the graph below, which shows the increase in tourism over ten years.

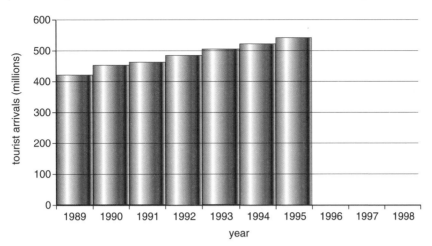

(a) Complete the graph using the data in this table.

1996	550 million
1997	580 million
1998	600 million

(3 marks)

(b) Describe the growth in global tourism shown by the graph.

....

.... (2 marks)

(c) Explain the reasons behind the growth in tourism.

....

....

....

.... (4 marks)

(d) Describe how the locations favoured by British tourists have changed over the past 100 years.

....

....

....

....

.... (6 marks)

Score   /15

How well did you do?

0–8 correct   Try again
9–15 correct   Getting there
16–23 correct   Good work
24–30 correct   Excellent!

TOTAL SCORE   /30

For more on this topic
see pages 64–65 of your Success Guide

TOURISM CASE STUDIES

Choose just one answer, a, b, c or d.

1 Where is Kenya located?
(a) North Africa
(b) East Africa
(c) South Africa
(d) West Africa (1 mark)

2 What is the average temperature in Kenya?
(a) 10°C
(b) 15°C
(c) 20°C
(d) 25°C (1 mark)

3 How many wet seasons are there in Kenya?
(a) One
(b) Two
(c) Three
(d) Four (1 mark)

4 Approximately how many Kenyans are employed in the tourist industry?
(a) 180,000
(b) 250,000
(c) 380,000
(d) 560,000 (1 mark)

5 Which of the following is a benefit of tourism in Kenya?
(a) The Maasai people have been removed from the National Parks
(b) Coral is taken home as a souvenir
(c) Tax is raised from tourism
(d) Minibuses cause soil erosion (1 mark)

Score /5

B Answer all parts of all questions.

1 Decide whether the statements below are true or false.

	True	False
(a) The Lake District is a National Park in south-west England	☐	☐
(b) National Parks are large urban areas which are protected from development	☐	☐
(c) National Parks were established in 1949 to preserve the beauty of the landscape	☐	☐
(d) The Lake District is an upland area shaped by glaciation	☐	☐
(e) The most popular tourist activity in the Lake District is sun bathing	☐	☐

(5 marks)

2 Label the five missing National Parks A–E on the map using the words on the right.

Northumberland
Lake District
North Yorks Moors
A
Peak District
E
B
Pembrokeshire Coast
D
Exmoor
New Forest
C

Brecon Beacons

Dartmoor

Norfolk Broads

Yorkshire Dales

Snowdonia

(5 marks)

Score /10

C These are GCSE-style questions. Answer all parts of the questions.

1 Study the resource below, which is an extract from a website about eco-tourism in Peru.

> **Eco-tourism in Peru**
>
> In the Tambopata Candamo Reserved Zone in south-eastern Peru, Rainforest Expeditions, a for-profit eco-tourism company formed by Peruvian conservationists, has entered into a joint eco-tourism venture with the Ese'eja Indian community to attract tourists to a biologically rich site boasting macaws, giant river otters and harpy eagles. The indigenous community provides labour, lodging and food for the project, and in return receives 60 per cent of the profits from the joint venture. Rainforest Expeditions requires a strong degree of local participation and gives the community equal decision-making power in the management of this unique endeavour.
>
>
>
> Both Rainforest Expeditions and the Ese'eja community realise that the success of their tourism venture depends on the protection of local wildlife resources. Accordingly, both sides are actively involved in research, management and conservation programs to protect the fragile ecosystem. Since its inception, the site has become a higly rated eco-tourism destination, developed innovative natural and cultural education programs, and played an increasingly important role in the conservation and sustainable development of the region.

(a) What is eco-tourism? ....

.... (2 marks)

(b) Where is the Tambopata Candamo Reserved Zone?

.... (2 marks)

(c) What attracts tourists to the Tambopata Candamo Reserved Zone?

....

....

....

.... (4 marks)

(d) How does Rainforest Expeditions manage tourism in a sustainable way?

....

....

....

....

....

.... (6 marks)

Score   /14

How well did you do?

0–7 correct   Try again
8–15 correct   Getting there
16–22 correct   Good work
23–29 correct   Excellent!

TOTAL SCORE   /29

For more on this topic
see pages 66–67 of your Success Guide

RESOURCES

A

Choose just one answer, a, b, c or d.

1 Which of the following is not a natural resource?
(a) Air   (b) Rock
(c) Plastic   (d) Soil   (1 mark)

2 How much waste is disposed of in the UK each year?
(a) 25 million tonnes   (b) 50 million tonnes
(c) 75 million tonnes   (d) 100 million tonnes
                       (1 mark)

3 Which of the following is not an objective agreed at the Earth Summit in Rio in 1992?
(a) To promote family planning
(b) To alleviate poverty
(c) To deplete resources
(d) To protect habitats and biodiversity
                       (1 mark)

4 Which part of the policy on sustainable development, agreed at the Earth Summit, aims to achieve sustainable development at a local level?
(a) Agenda 21
(b) Agenda 35
(c) Agenda 50
(d) Agenda 92   (1 mark)

5 How much waste is recycled in the UK?
(a) 3%
(b) 8%
(c) 18%
(d) 30%   (1 mark)

Score   /5

B

Answer all parts of all questions.

1 Classify the following resources as either renewable or non-renewable.

(a) Water.
(b) Timber.
(c) Soil.
(d) Coal.
(e) Iron ore.
(f) Gas.

Renewable resources	Non-renewable resources

                       (6 marks)

2 Resource substitution means replacing one resource with another. Complete the table below to show how the four resources may be substituted with another.

Resource	Substitute
Rubber	
Cotton	
Petrol	
Tin cans	

                       (4 marks)

Score   /10

C **These are GCSE-style questions. Answer all parts of the questions.**

1 Study the diagram below, which shows a recycling bank.

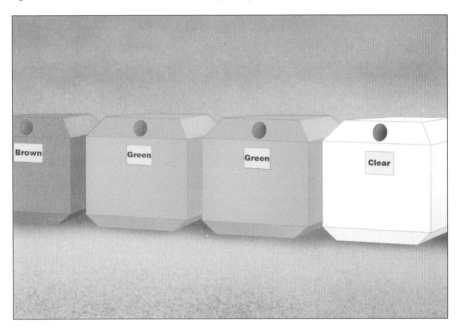

Brown Green Green Clear

(a) What is meant by the term 'recycling'? ....
.... (2 marks)

(b) What things can usually be recycled in the UK? ....
.... (4 marks)

(c) How does recycling benefit the environment?
....
....
....
.... (4 marks)

(d) Why might some people object to having a recycling bank sited close to their home?
....
....
.... (3 marks)

(e) What happens to the majority of waste in the UK?
....
.... (2 marks)

Score   /15

How well did you do?

0–8 correct	Try again
9–15 correct	Getting there
16–23 correct	Good work
24–30 correct	Excellent!

TOTAL SCORE   /30

**For more on this topic
see pages 68–69 of your Success Guide**

ENERGY

A

Choose just one answer, a, b, c or d.

1 What percentage of the world's energy is consumed by MEDCs?
(a) 20%   (b) 40%
(c) 60%   (d) 80%   (1 mark)

2 How much is the global energy consumption expected to increase by 2020?
(a) 25%
(b) 50%
(c) 75%
(d) 100%   (1 mark)

3 Which of the following is a fossil fuel?
(a) Solar energy
(b) Coal
(c) Geothermal energy
(d) Wood   (1 mark)

4 What percentage of the world's energy is provided by fossil fuels?
(a) 25%
(b) 47%
(c) 60%
(d) 90%   (1 mark)

5 Which of the following is a form of renewable energy?
(a) Coal
(b) Oil
(c) Tidal energy
(d) Gas   (1 mark)

Score   /5

B

Answer all parts of all questions.

1 Complete the following sentences about energy using the numbers on the right.

(a) Oil is formed from the remains of tiny sea creatures that lived .... million years ago. | 45

(b) Known oil reserves will last for another .... years. | 300

(c) Coal is rock formed from the remains of trees that are .... million years old. | 400

(d) Known coal reserves will last for another ....years. | 200

(e) Wind turbine blades turn at up to ....kilometres per hour. | 300

(5 marks)

2 Cross out the incorrect words in the sentences below.

(a) Fossil fuels are a finite/infinite resource.

(b) The known reserves of uranium will last for over 1,000/2,000 years.

(c) Wind power is most suitable in lowland/upland areas.

(d) Hydroelectric power is most suitable in areas of permeable/impermeable rock.

(e) Electricity is a type of primary/secondary energy.

(5 marks)

Score   /10

C These are GCSE-style questions. Answer all parts of the questions.

1 Study the map, which shows the amount of energy used by different countries.

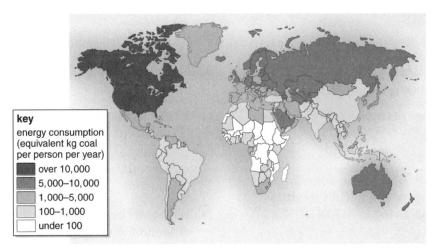

key
energy consumption
(equivalent kg coal
per person per year)

- over 10,000
- 5,000–10,000
- 1,000–5,000
- 100–1,000
- under 100

(a) Describe the pattern of energy usage shown by the map.

....

....

....

.... (4 marks)

(b) Explain why the amount of energy consumed globally will change over the next

20 years..

....

....

.... (4 marks)

(c) With reference to an example you have studied, describe how renewable resources

may be used to produce electricity. ....

....

.... (3 marks)

(d) What are the advantages and disadvantages of the type of renewable energy you

described in **(c)**? ....

....

....

.... (4 marks)

Score   /15

How well did you do?

 0–8 correct   Try again
9–15 correct   Getting there
6–23 correct   Good work
4–30 correct   Excellent!

TOTAL SCORE   /30

**For more on this topic
see pages 70–71 of your Success Guide**

DEVELOPMENT

A

Choose just one answer, a, b, c or d.

1 What percentage of the world's population live in MEDCs?
(a) 10%   (b) 20%
(c) 30%   (d) 40%   (1 mark)

2 What percentage of the world's wealth is owned by people living in MEDCs?
(a) 20%
(b) 40%
(c) 60%
(d) 80%   (1 mark)

3 Which of the following is an MEDC?
(a) Norway
(b) Mexico
(c) Thailand
(d) Egypt   (1 mark)

4 Which of the following is an LEDC?
(a) Australia
(b) India
(c) Canada
(d) Japan   (1 mark)

5 Which of the following is not a good indicator of level of development?
(a) Death rate
(b) Population
(c) Life expectancy
(d) Education   (1 mark)

Score   /5

B

Answer all parts of all questions.

1 Classify the following development projects as either prestige projects or appropriate technology projects.

(a) Dam.   (b) Tube well.   (c) Toilet block.   (d) Motorway.   (e) Airport.   (f) Kerosene cooking stove.

Prestige projects	Appropriate technology projects

(6 marks)

2 Add the following labels to the diagram below to illustrate the cycle of underdevelopment.

(a) Few exports, illiteracy and poor health.

(b) LEDC.

(c) Lack of industry, education and healthcare.

(d) Not enough money to invest in infrastructure.

(4 marks)

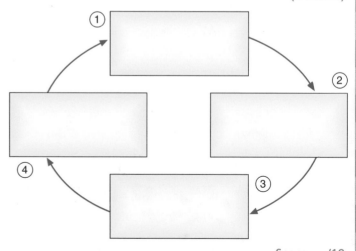

Score   /10

C These are GCSE-style questions. Answer all parts of the questions.

1 Study the scattergraph, which shows the relationship between Gross National Product (GNP) per capita and population per doctor.

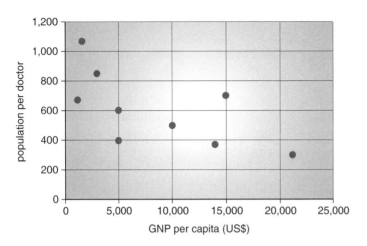

(a) What is meant by the term 'development'?

....

....

....

....

(2 marks)

(b) Complete the scattergraph using the data for the UK and the USA in the table below. (2 marks)

Country	GNP per capita (US$)	Population per doctor
UK	18,000	300
USA	25,000	400

(c) Add a line of best fit to the scattergraph. (1 mark)

(d) Describe the relationship shown by the graph. ....

....

.... (3 marks)

(e) Suggest reasons to explain the relationship shown by the graph.

....

....

....

.... (4 marks)

(f) Explain why GNP per capita is not a sufficient measure of development on its own.

....

....

.... (3 marks)

Score   /15

How well did you do?

0–8 correct   Try again
9–15 correct   Getting there
16–23 correct Good work
24–30 correct Excellent!

TOTAL SCORE   /30

For more on this topic see pages 72–73 of your Success Guide

TRADE AND AID

A

Choose just one answer, a, b, c or d.

1 Which of the following words best describes the process of goods being sold by a country?
(a) Import　　　(b) Export
(c) Trade　　　(d) Sale　　(1 mark)

2 Which of the following is not a benefit of fair trade?
(a) Minimum wages
(b) Safe working conditions
(c) Child labour
(d) Protection for the environment　(1 mark)

3 Which of the following is not a manufactured product?
(a) Sugar cane　　(b) Tinned beef
(c) Circuit boards　(d) Instant coffee
(1 mark)

4 What percentage of a country's GNP do the United Nations recommend is spent on aid?
(a) 0.7%
(b) 7%
(c) 27%
(d) 70%　　(1 mark)

5 What type of aid is it when the recipient country must agree to spend money on goods produced in the donor country?
(a) Bilateral aid
(b) Emergency aid
(c) NGO aid
(d) Tied aid　　(1 mark)

Score　/5

B

Answer all parts of all questions.

1 Match the following descriptions with the correct type of international aid.

(a) WaterAid supplies tube wells in Bangladesh ....

(b) Food supplies to Ethiopia in time of famine ....

(c) A loan from the World Bank to Turkey ....

(d) Doctors from Italy spend a year training doctors in Uganda ....

(e) A £2 million donation from the UK to Afghanistan ....

emergency aid

long-term aid

multilateral aid

bilateral aid

NGO aid

(5 marks)

2 Decide whether the statements below are true or false

	True	False
(a) Food aid can put local farmers out of business	☐	☐
(b) Aid is frequently a loan rather than a donation	☐	☐
(c) The largest donors of aid are China and Egypt	☐	☐
(d) LEDCs are earning more each year as the price of raw materials rises	☐	☐
(e) Fair trade benefits people who live in LEDCs	☐	☐

(5 marks)

Score　/10

70

These are GCSE-style questions. Answer all parts of the questions.

1 Study the map, which shows the pattern of world trade.

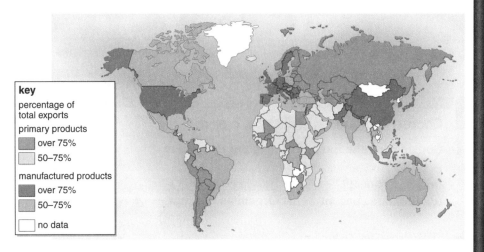

key

percentage of total exports

primary products

☐ over 75%

☐ 50–75%

manufactured products

☐ over 75%

☐ 50–75%

☐ no data

(a) What is meant by the term 'trade'? ....

.... (2 marks)

(b) Describe the distribution of countries whose exports are over 75% manufactured goods.

....

.... (2 marks)

(c) Suggest reasons to explain the distribution you described in **(b)**.

....

.... (2 marks)

(d) Describe the distribution of countries whose exports are over 75% primary products.

....

.... (2 marks)

(e) Suggest reasons to explain the distribution you described in **(d)**.

....

.... (2 marks)

(f) What are the advantages and disadvantages of this pattern of trade?

....

....

....

....

.... (5 marks)

Score   /15

How well did you do?

0–8 correct   Try again

9–15 correct   Getting there

16–23 correct   Good work

24–30 correct   Excellent!

TOTAL SCORE   /30

For more on this topic see pages 74–75 of your Success Guide

ECOSYSTEMS

A Choose just one answer, a, b, c or d.

1 Considering the Earth as one giant ecosystem is called the
(a) Gaia concept   (b) Biome concept
(c) Biomass concept   (d) Organism concept
(1 mark)

2 Deciduous woodland ecosystems consist of
(a) Dense evergreen trees
(b) Short plants such as moss and heather
(c) Hundreds of different species of very tall trees
(d) Trees that shed their leaves in winter
(1 mark)

3 Tropical grassland ecosystems consist of
(a) Grasses up to two metres tall
(b) Short grasses and heather
(c) Grasses up to five metres tall
(d) Drought-resistant plants such as cacti
(1 mark)

4 Which word best describes an animal which eats plants?
(a) Vegetarian
(b) Herbivore
(c) Carnivore
(d) Omnivore
(1 mark)

5 Which of the following is a tertiary consumer?
(a) Killer whale
(b) Blackbird
(c) Rabbit
(d) Snail
(1 mark)

Score   /5

B Answer all parts of all questions.

1 Label the map below to show the location of ecosystems A–H.

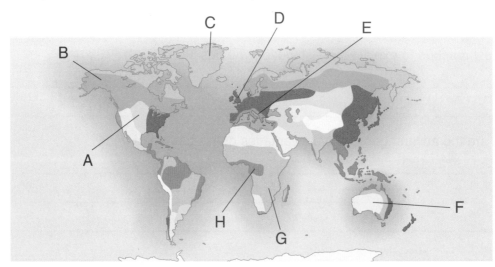

(8 marks)

2 Name two factors which control the type of ecosystem that develops in an area.

....

....
(2 marks)

Score   /10

C **These are GCSE-style questions. Answer all parts of the questions.**

1 Study the diagram, which shows a simplified food web in a deciduous woodland ecosystem.

(a) What is the source of energy in any ecosystem?

....

....

....

....

(1 mark)

(b) What is the difference between a food web and a food chain?

....

.... (2 marks)

(c) Name two primary consumers shown in the diagram.

....

.... (2 marks)

(d) Each step of the food chain is called a trophic level. At what trophic level is the fox

shown in the diagram? .... (1 mark)

(e) Explain why the number of living organisms in an ecosystem decreases with each

trophic level. ....

....

....

.... (4 marks)

(f) Describe how people have altered energy flows and nutrient cycles in an ecosystem you have studied.

....

....

....

.... (5 marks)

Score   /15

ow well did you do?

–8 correct   Try again
15 correct   Getting there
23 correct   Good work
30 correct   Excellent!

TOTAL SCORE   /30

For more on this topic
see pages 82–83 of your Success Guide

GLOBAL ENVIRONMENTS

A

Choose just one answer, a, b, c or d.

1 In which of the following countries would you find coniferous forest?
(a) Australia　　(b) Canada
(c) Kenya　　(d) Brazil　　(1 mark)

2 What is the average temperature in coniferous forest ecosystems in January?
(a) –10°C　　(b) –18°C
(c) –20°C　　(d) –28°C　　(1 mark)

3 What type of soil is found in coniferous forest ecosystems?
(a) Podsol
(b) Red clay
(c) Brown earth
(d) Chernozem　　(1 mark)

4 Which of the following is not a characteristic of coniferous trees?
(a) Thin bark
(b) Shallow roots
(c) Seeds in cones
(d) Evergreen　　(1 mark)

5 Which of the following is not a species of coniferous tree?
(a) Spruce
(b) Fir
(c) Oak
(d) Pine　　(1 mark)

Score　/5

B

Answer all parts of all questions.

1 Cross out the incorrect words in the sentences below.

(a) Tropical rainforests are located 5°/20° north and south of the equator.

(b) Red clay/podsol soils are found in tropical rainforests.

(c) Tropical rainforests have high/low humidity.

(d) Tropical rainforests have weekly/daily rainfall.

(e) Tropical rainforests are at risk from afforestation/deforestation.　　(5 marks)

2 Label the diagram of tropical rainforest soil with the words below.

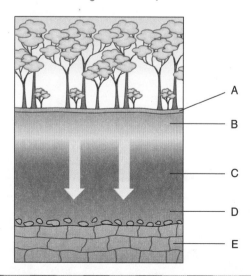

A
B
C
D
E

bedrock

leaching

litter

humus

weathering

(5 marks)

Score　/10

C **These are GCSE-style questions. Answer all parts of the questions.**

1 Study the diagram below, which shows a tropical grassland.

(a) Where in the world are tropical grasslands located?

....

.... (2 marks)

(b) Describe the vegetation shown in the illustration.

....

....

.... (3 marks)

(c) Describe the climate associated with tropical grassland ecosystems.

....

....

....

.... (4 marks)

(d) Describe and explain how tropical grassland vegetation is adapted to the climate.

....

....

....

....

....

.... (6 marks)

Score   /15

How well did you do?

0–8 correct   Try again
9–15 correct   Getting there
5–23 correct   Good work
4–30 correct   Excellent!

TOTAL SCORE   /30

**For more on this topic
see pages 84–85 of your Success Guide**

GLOBAL WARMING

A

Choose just one answer, a, b, c or d.

1 Which of the following is not a greenhouse gas?
(a) Water vapour   (b) Carbon dioxide
(c) Nitrogen   (d) Methane   (1 mark)

2 Which of the following countries releases the most greenhouse gases?
(a) USA
(b) India
(c) China
(d) Russia   (1 mark)

3 How much has the average global temperature increased in the last 100 years?
(a) 0.6°C
(b) 1°C
(c) 1.6°C
(d) 6°C   (1 mark)

4 Which of the following is not a possible effect of global warming on the UK?
(a) Warmer summers
(b) Higher crop yields
(c) Glaciers melting
(d) More forest fires   (1 mark)

5 Which of the following was the location of a world summit on global climate change?
(a) New York
(b) Kyoto
(c) London
(d) Sydney   (1 mark)

Score   /5

B

Answer all parts of all questions.

1 Decide whether the statements below are true or false.

(a) By the year 2100 the average global temperature could increase by 5.8°C

(b) In the last 100 years sea level has risen by 20 cm

(c) The average global temperature is 15°C

(d) In the USA the average amount of carbon dioxide emitted per person each year is 6.6 tonnes

(e) The more economically developed countries have agreed to reduce greenhouse gas emissions to 5% below 1990 levels.

True   False

(5 marks)

2 Use the map below to identify the maximum temperature change which may occur in the following countries as a result of global warming.

(a) UK ....

(b) France ....

(c) Spain ....

(d) Switzerland ....

(e) Iceland ....

Forecast change in temperature by 2050

key
°C change
7
5
4
3
2
1

Score   /10

C **These are GCSE-style questions. Answer all parts of the questions.**

1 Study the cartoon, which is about an international conference on global warming.

(a) What is the difference between the greenhouse effect and global warming?

....

.... (2 marks)

(b) State three pieces of evidence which suggest that global warming is occurring.

....

....

.... (3 marks)

(c) Explain what is meant by the cartoon. ....

....

....

.... (4 marks)

(d) Explain the causes of global warming under the following headings.

Fossil fuels ....

....

Deforestation ....

....

Methane ....

.... (6 marks)

Score   /15

How well did you do?

0–8 correct   Try again
9–15 correct   Getting there
16–23 correct Good work
24–30 correct Excellent!

TOTAL SCORE   /30

For more on this topic
see pages 86–87 of your Success Guide

ACID RAIN

A

Choose just one answer, a, b, c or d.

1 When was the problem of acid rain first identified?
(a) 1950s   (b) 1960s
(c) 1970s   (d) 1980s   (1 mark)

2 How far can acid rain travel from its source?
(a) 1,000 km
(b) 2,000 km
(c) 3,000 km
(d) 4,000 km   (1 mark)

3 How far can acid deposition travel from its source?
(a) 100 km
(b) 150 km
(c) 200 km
(d) 250 km   (1 mark)

4 Which of the following countries in Europe has been badly affected by acid rain?
(a) Spain
(b) Italy
(c) Greece
(d) Poland   (1 mark)

5 By how much has the UK agreed to reduce its emissions of pollution which cause acid rain?
(a) 20%
(b) 40%
(c) 60%
(d) 80%   (1 mark)

Score   /5

B

Answer all parts of all questions.

1 Describe the effects of acid rain for each of the key words below.

(a) Soil ....

(b) Trees ....

(c) Lakes ....

(d) Water supplies ....

(e) Buildings .... (5 marks)

2 Decide whether the statements below are true or false.

	True	False
(a) Catalytic converters in cars increase acid rain	☐	☐
(b) Adding lime to lakes reduces the acidity of the water	☐	☐
(c) The Taj Mahal in India is being damaged by acid rain	☐	☐
(d) Acid rain contains citric and nitric acid	☐	☐
(e) Filters can be added to power station chimneys to reduce acid rain	☐	☐

(5 marks)

Score   /10

C These are GCSE-style questions. Answer all parts of the questions.

1 Study the map, which shows the acidity of rain falling on the USA.

(a) What is acid rain?

....

....

....

....

....

....

....

....

(2 marks)

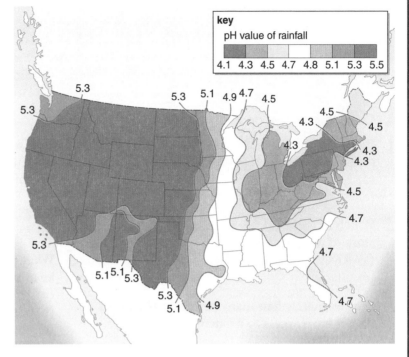

key
pH value of rainfall
4.1 4.3 4.5 4.7 4.8 5.1 5.3 5.5

(b) Describe the distribution of acid rain falling in the USA.

....

....

....

....
(4 marks)

(c) Explain what causes acid rain. ....

....

....

....
(4 marks)

(d) Suggest reasons to explain the distribution of acid rain in the USA.

....

....
(2 marks)

(e) Explain why acid rain may cause conflict between countries.

....

....

....
(3 marks)

Score   /15

How well did you do?

0–8 correct   Try again
9–15 correct   Getting there
16–23 correct Good work
24–30 correct Excellent!

TOTAL SCORE   /30

For more on this topic
see page 86 of your Success Guide

USE AND ABUSE OF THE ENVIRONMENT – WATER

A

Choose just one answer, a, b, c or d.

1 By how many times has the global demand for water increased in the past **100** years?
(**a**) 2 times   (**b**) 4 times
(**c**) 6 times   (**d**) 8 times   (1 mark)

2 Which of the following is an underground store of water?
(**a**) River   (**b**) Reservoir
(**c**) Glacier   (**d**) Aquifer   (1 mark)

3 Approximately how many people in the world do not have access to a safe water supply?
(**a**) 1 million
(**b**) 100 million
(**c**) 1 billion
(**d**) 2 billion   (1 mark)

4 How many people die each day from diseases caused by dirty water?
(**a**) 250
(**b**) 2,500
(**c**) 25,000
(**d**) 250,000   (1 mark)

5 What proportion of the world's population will be at risk of water shortage by the year 2025?
(**a**) 11%
(**b**) 33%
(**c**) 66%
(**d**) 99%   (1 mark)

Score   /5

B

Answer all parts of all questions.

1 (a) Use the data in the table below to draw a scattergraph to show the link between population growth and water use.   (5 marks)

Year	Population (billions)	Water use (km^3)
1910	1.75	900
1920	1.86	1,000
1930	2.07	1,100
1940	2.30	1,300
1950	2.52	1,700
1960	3.02	2,500
1970	3.70	3,500
1980	4.44	4,300
1990	5.27	5,500
2000	6.06	7,200

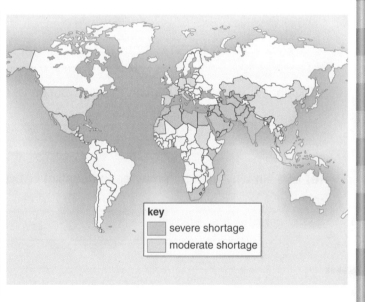

key
severe shortage
moderate shortage

(b) Add a line of best fit to the scattergraph.   (1 mark)

(c) Describe the relationship shown by the graph. _____

_____ (2 marks)

Score   /8

These are GCSE-style questions. Answer all parts of the questions.

1 Study the map, which shows countries predicted by the United Nations to have a water shortage by 2025.

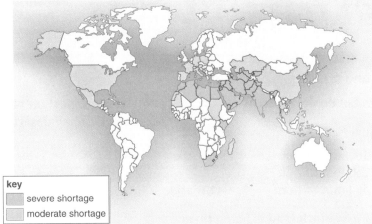

key
severe shortage
moderate shortage

(a) Describe the distribution of countries which are predicted to have a moderate

shortage of water by 2025. ....

.... (2 marks)

(b) Describe the distribution of countries which are predicted to have a severe

shortage of water by 2025. ....

.... (2 marks)

(c) Explain why the areas you described in **(a)** and **(b)** are likely to experience a

shortage of water. ....

....

....

....

....

.... (6 marks)

(d) Suggest what might be done to ensure a sustainable water supply in the future.

....

....

....

....

.... (5 marks)

Score   /15

How well did you do?

0–7 correct   Try again
8–14 correct   Getting there
15–21 correct   Good work
22–28 correct   Excellent!

TOTAL SCORE   /28

For more on this topic
see page 88 of your Success Guide

USE AND ABUSE OF THE ENVIRONMENT – LAND

A Choose just one answer, a, b, c or d.

1 How much rainfall do desert areas receive each year?
(a) No rain at all
(b) Less than 100 mm of rain
(c) Less than 250 mm of rain
(d) Less than 500 mm of rain   (1 mark)

2 Approximately how much land is being turned into desert each year?
(a) 5 million hectares   (b) 8 million hectares
(c) 12 million hectares (d) 15 million hectares
                                           (1 mark)

3 Which area in the world is most at risk from desertification?
(a) Australia   (b) Middle east
(c) USA   (d) North Africa
                                           (1 mark)

4 What proportion of the world's countries are experiencing desertification?
(a) 11%
(b) 33%
(c) 66%
(d) 99%   (1 mark)

5 What is the average length of time taken for 1 cm of soil to develop?
(a) 100 years
(b) 200 years
(c) 500 years
(d) 1,000 years   (1 mark)

Score   /5

B Answer all parts of all questions.

1 Classify the following effects of desertification as either short term or long term.

(a) Crop failure.

(b) Refugees.

(c) Soil erosion.

(d) Famine.

(e) Disease.

(f) Urbanisation.

Short-term effects	Long-term effects

(6 marks)

2 Explain how desertification may be slowed or prevented using the following methods.

(a) Diguettes ....

....

(b) Contour ploughing ....

....

(c) Tree planting ....

....

(d) Genetically modified crops ....

....   (4 marks)

Score   /10

C

These are GCSE-style questions. Answer all parts of the questions.

1 Study the map, which shows areas at risk of desertification.

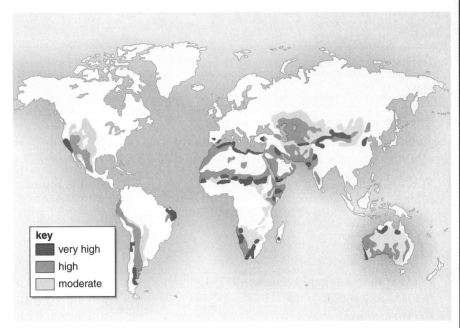

key
- very high
- high
- moderate

(a) What is desertification? .... (1 mark)

(b) Describe the distribution of areas at risk from desertification.

....

....

....

.... (4 marks)

(c) Explain why deserts are expanding using the key words below.

Climate change ....

.... (2 marks)

Population growth ....

.... (2 marks)

Overgrazing ....

.... (2 marks)

Irrigation ....

.... (2 marks)

Deforestation ....

.... (2 marks)

Score   /15

How well did you do?

0–8 correct   Try again
9–15 correct   Getting there
6–23 correct   Good work
4–30 correct   Excellent!

TOTAL SCORE   /30

For more on this topic
see pages 88–89 of your Success Guide

MAP SKILLS

A

Choose just one answer, a, b, c or d.

The following questions refer to the Ordnance Survey Map extract and key on pages 86 and 87.

1 What is found at grid reference 050849?
(a) Windmill
(b) Beacon
(c) Lighthouse
(d) TV mast   (1 mark)

2 What is found at grid reference 987917?
(a) Railway station
(b) Bus station
(c) Youth hostel
(d) Main road   (1 mark)

3 What is found at grid reference 029932?
(a) Leisure centre
(b) College

(c) School
(d) Hospital   (1 mark)

4 What is found at grid reference 973878?
(a) Caravan site
(b) Car park
(c) Camp site
(d) Picnic site   (1 mark)

5 What is found at grid reference 021914?
(a) Church with a spire
(b) Church with a tower
(c) Church
(d) Tower   (1 mark)

Score   /5

B

Answer all parts of all questions.

1 Use this sketch map of the Ordnance Survey map on page 87 to answer the following questions.

(a) What is the coastal landform shown in the sketch map?

....   (1 mark)

(b) Add the following labels to the sketch map.

| sand dunes | salt marsh | mixed woodland | beach |

(4 marks)

Score   /5

These are GCSE-style questions. You should refer to the Ordnance Survey map extract and key on pages 86 and 87.

1 How many square kilometres are covered by the map extract? .... (1 mark)

2 If you were sailing from Long Island to Furzey Island, in which direction would you be travelling? .... (1 mark)

3 What is the distance covered by the ferry route from Poole to Brownsea Island?

.... (1 mark)

4 What is the highest point on Green Island? .... (1 mark)

5 What evidence is there in grid square 9994 that the area has been inhabited for a long time? .... (1 mark)

6 Describe the differences in housing between grid squares 0094 and 0492.

....

.... (2 marks)

7 Describe the differences in land use between the north and the south of the map.

....

....

.... (4 marks)

8 What evidence is there of industry in the southern half of the map?

.... (1 mark)

9 What evidence is there that Poole Harbour is a drowned river valley (ria)?

....

.... (2 marks)

10 How long is the ferry journey from Poole to St Malo?

.... (1 mark)

11 Why is it not possible to take a ferry from Poole to Jersey in December?

.... (1 mark)

12 What evidence is there on the map that Poole is a tourist destination?

....

....

.... (4 marks)

Score   /20

How well did you do?
0–8 correct   Try again
9–15 correct   Getting there
16–23 correct Good work
24–30 correct Excellent!

TOTAL SCORE   /30

For more on this topic
see pages 92–93 of your Success Guide

ORDNANCE SURVEY MAP EXTRACT

Opposite is an Ordnance Survey map extract of Poole.

This is to be used to answer the questions on pages 84 and 85.

LAND FEATURES

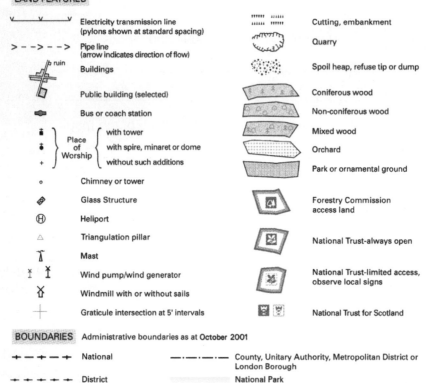

Electricity transmission line (pylons shown at standard spacing)	Cutting, embankment
Pipe line (arrow indicates direction of flow)	Quarry
Buildings	Spoil heap, refuse tip or dump
Public building (selected)	Coniferous wood
Bus or coach station	Non-coniferous wood
Place of Worship — with tower / with spire, minaret or dome / without such additions	Mixed wood
	Orchard
Chimney or tower	Park or ornamental ground
Glass Structure	Forestry Commission access land
Heliport	
Triangulation pillar	National Trust-always open
Mast	
Wind pump/wind generator	National Trust-limited access, observe local signs
Windmill with or without sails	
Graticule intersection at 5' intervals	National Trust for Scotland

BOUNDARIES   Administrative boundaries as at October 2001

+ — + — +   National

+ — + — +   District

— · — · —   County, Unitary Authority, Metropolitan District or London Borough

National Park

ABBREVIATIONS

CH	Clubhouse	CG	Coastguard
MS	Milestone	P	Post office
PC	Public convenience (in rural area)	MP	Milepost
TH	Town Hall, Guildhall or equivalent	PH	Public house

ARCHAEOLOGICAL AND HISTORICAL INFORMATION

+ Site of monument   ⚔ Battlefield (with date)   VILLA   Roman

· ○ Stone monument   ☆ ···· Visible earthwork   Castle   Non-Roman

Information provided by English Heritage for England and the Royal Commissions on the Ancient and Historical Monuments for Scotland and Wales

HEIGHTS

——50——   Contours are at 10 metres vertical interval

144   Heights are to the nearest metre above mean sea level

Heights shown close to a triangulation pillar refer to the ground at the base of the pillar and not necessarily to the summit

HOW TO GIVE A NATIONAL GRID REFERENCE TO NEAREST 100 METRES

SAMPLE POINT: **Hordle Grange**

1. Read letters identifying 100 000 metre square in which the point lies ....SZ

2. FIRST QUOTE EASTINGS
Locate first VERTICAL grid line to LEFT of point and read LARGE figures labelling the line either in the top or bottom margin or on the line itself 26
Estimate tenths from grid line to point 5

3. AND THEN QUOTE NORTHINGS
Locate first HORIZONTAL grid line BELOW point and read LARGE figures labelling the line either in the left or right margin or on the line itself 96
Estimate tenths from grid line to point...3

SAMPLE REFERENCE   SZ 265 963
For local referencing grid letters may be omitted

IGNORE the SMALLER figures of the grid number at the corner of the map. These are for fine the full coordinates. Use ONLY the LARGER figure of the grid number. EXAMPLE: ³89⁰⁰

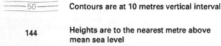

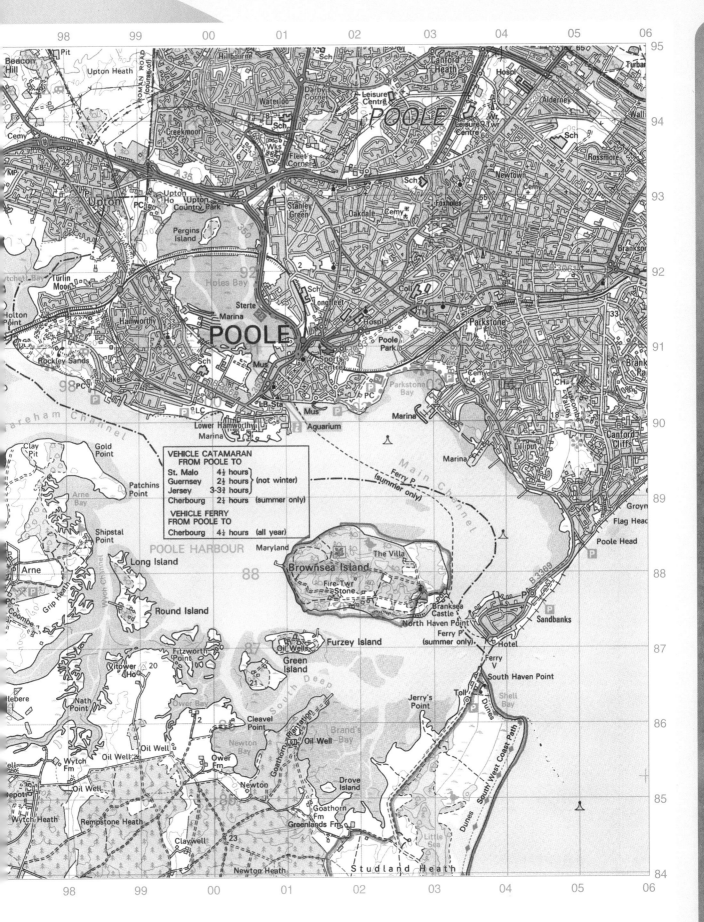

VEHICLE CATAMARAN FROM POOLE TO

St. Malo	4½ hours	
Guernsey	2¼ hours	(not winter)
Jersey	3-3¼ hours	
Cherbourg	2¼ hours	(summer only)

VEHICLE FERRY FROM POOLE TO

Cherbourg	4¼ hours	(all year)

POOLE

POOLE HARBOUR

Brownsea Island

Studland Heath

MIXED GCSE-STYLE QUESTIONS

Tectonic activity

1 Label features A–E on the diagram.

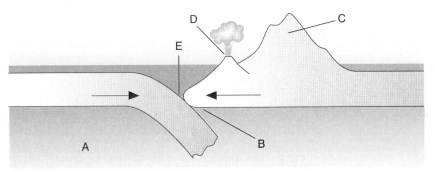

(5 marks)

2 (a) Name an area of fold mountains. (1 mark)

(b) Explain how fold mountains are formed. (4 marks)

Total score   /10

Landforms

1 Study the sketch, which shows
a landform found in a granite area.

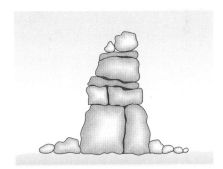

(a) Identify the landform. (1 mark)

(b) Describe the appearance of the landform. (3 marks)

(c) Explain briefly how the landform is formed. (3 marks)

(d) Describe how people use granite areas. (3 marks)

Total score   /10

Rivers

1 Label features A–E on the diagram. (5 marks)

2 Explain how an oxbow lake is formed.
You may use diagrams to help you.

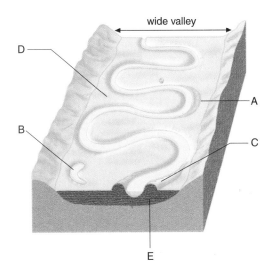

(5 marks)

Total score   /10

Coasts

1 Label features A–E on the diagram. (5 marks)

2 (a) What is a spit? (1 mark)

(b) Explain how spits are formed. (4 marks)

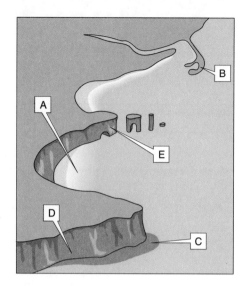

Total score /10

Glaciation

1 Label processes and features A–E on the diagram. (5 marks)

2 (a) What is a corrie? (1 mark)

(b) Explain how a corrie is formed. (4 marks)

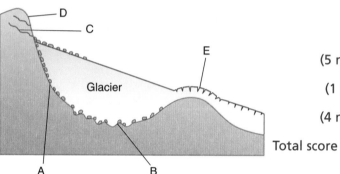

Glacier

Total score /10

Weather and climate

1 Study the map, which shows the average temperatures for the UK in July.

(a) What is the name for lines on a weather map which show areas of equal temperature? (1 mark)

(b) What is the average temperature in London in July? (1 mark)

(c) Describe the pattern of temperatures shown by the map. (4 marks)

(d) Explain the pattern of temperatures shown on the map. (4 marks)

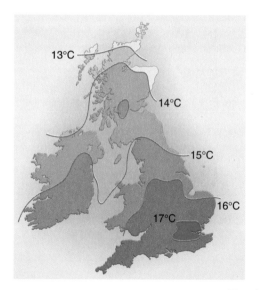

13°C
14°C
15°C
16°C
17°C

Total score /10

Population

1 Study the map, which shows the global population distribution.

(a) What is meant by the term 'population distribution'? (1 mark)

(b) Describe the pattern of population distribution shown by the map. (4 marks)

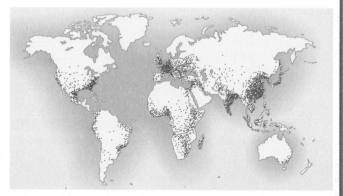

2 With reference to an example you have studied, explain how governments may try to control population growth.

(5 marks)

Total score   /10

Settlement

1 Study the map of Paris.

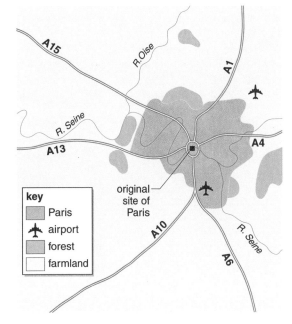

(a) When was Paris first settled?   (1 mark)

(b) What is the population of Paris?   (1 mark)

(c) Label the map of Paris to explain its original site.   (5 marks)

(d) Describe the location of Paris today.

(3 marks)

Total score   /10

Agriculture

1 Study the photograph, which shows a river that has been affected by nitrate pollution.

(a) Describe the scene in the photograph.   (2 marks)

(b) Describe how and why farmers use nitrates.   (2 marks)

(c) Explain how nitrate pollution can damage the environment.   (6 marks)

Total score   /10

Industry

1 Study the map, which shows the distribution of the UK's modern industries.

(a) What is meant by the term 'modern industry'? (2 marks)

(b) Modern industries may be described as footloose. What does this mean? (2 marks)

(c) Describe the distribution of modern industry, as shown by the map. (3 marks)

(d) Suggest reasons to explain the distribution you have described in **(c)**. (3 marks)

Total score   /10

Tourism

1 Study the map of Kenya. Kenya developed a thriving tourist industry during the 1990s.

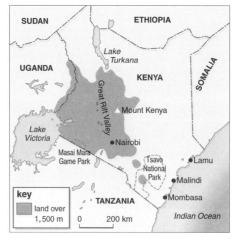

(a) Where is Kenya located? (1 mark)

(b) What is the capital city of Kenya? (1 mark)

(c) Describe the relief in Kenya. (3 marks)

(d) Name two ways in which tourism has benefited Kenya. (2 marks)

(e) Describe how tourism in Kenya has led to conflicts in some areas. (3 marks)

Total score   /10

Resources

1 Label features A–E on the diagram. (5 marks)

2 (a) Why are oil and gas known as fossil fuels?
(1 mark)

(b) Describe the advantages and disadvantages of oil and gas as a source of energy. (4 marks)

Total score   /10

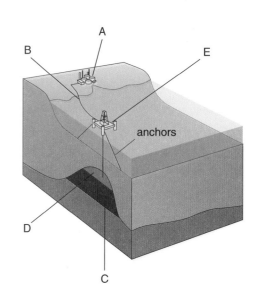

Development

1 Study the map, which shows international aid donors and recipients.

(a) Define the term 'international aid'. **(2 marks)**

(b) Describe the location of the world's most generous aid providers **(2 marks)**

(c) Describe the location of the world's largest receivers of international aid. **(2 marks)**

(d) What are the advantages and disadvantages of aid? **(4 marks)**

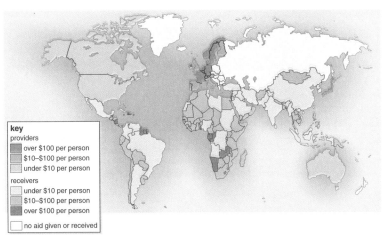

key

providers

over $100 per person
$10–$100 per person
under $10 per person

receivers

under $10 per person
$10–$100 per person
over $100 per person

no aid given or received

Total score   /10

Ecosystems

1 Label features A–E on the diagram of a podsoil soil. **(5 marks)**

2 (a) Describe the location of coniferous forests. **(2 marks)**

(b) Describe the climate associated with areas of coniferous forest. **(3 marks)**

Total score   /10

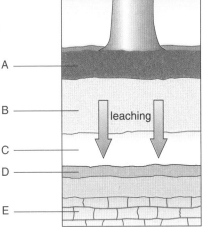

A

B   leaching

C

D

E

Global environmental concerns

1 Study the satellite image, which shows the hole in the ozone layer.

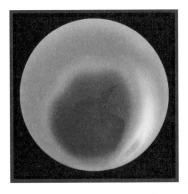

(a) Over which continent is the hole in the ozone layer? **(1 mark)**

(b) What function does the ozone layer serve? **(2 marks)**

(c) What has led to the formation of the hole in the ozone layer? **(3 marks)**

(d) What are the possible consequences of the hole in the ozone layer? **(4 marks)**

Total score   /10

MIXED QUESTIONS – ANSWERS

Tectonic activity

1 A = Mantle
B = Subduction zone
C = Fold mountains
D = Volcano
E = Ocean trench

2 (a) e.g. Alps, Himalayas, Rockies

(b) Two tectonic plates collide (1), pressure causes continental crust (1) to buckle upwards (1), folding and faulting to form mountains (1), continental crust is not dense enough to sink into the mantle (1)

Landforms

1 (a) Tor

(b) Large blocks of rock (1), appear to be balanced on top of each other (1), rounded edges (1), horizontal cracks (1), vertical cracks (1)

(c) Formed from granite (1), physical weathering, e.g. freeze–thaw (1) and chemical weathering, e.g. hydrolysis (1) have worn away the joints to leave behind large blocks of rock (1)

(d) Sheep and cattle grazing (1), building stone (1), china clay (1), tourism (1)

Rivers

1 A = Meander
B = Ox-bow lake
C = Levée
D = Flood plain
E = Alluvium

2 *Level 1* (1–2) basic answer, describes rather than explains, *Level 2* (3–4) clear answer, explains formation in terms of erosion and deposition, *Level 3* (5) detailed answer, explains formation in terms of erosion and deposition linked to fastest and slowest flow in logical sequence, e.g. river flows fastest on outside bend, more energy, more erosion, during a period of high flow narrow neck of land separating meanders is eroded, river breaks through and follows shorter, steeper, course, slow flow in old meander, low energy, deposition, meander becomes cut off

Coasts

1 A = Bay
B = Spit
C = Wave-cut platform
D = Cliff
E = Headland

2 (a) Curved beach of sand and pebbles extending out into the sea

(b) *Level 1* (1–2) basic answer, beach material is deposited and builds up to form a spit, *Level 2* (3–4) clear answer, longshore drift moves material along the coast, depositing it at a river mouth or where the coast changes direction

Glaciation

1 A = Plucking
B = Abrasion
C = Freeze–thaw weathering
D = Backwall
E = Crevasses

2 (a) Deep circular hollow near mountain summit where glaciers are formed

(b) *Level 1* (1–2) basic answer, mainly descriptive, e.g. ice erodes the land as the glacier moves downhill, *Level 2* (3–4) clear answer, explanatory, e.g. snow collects in hollows, compacted, turned to ice, slides downhill, eroding by abrasion and plucking, removes rock, steepens sides and deepens floor

Weather and climate

1 (a) Isotherms

(b) 17°C

(c) Temperatures decrease with latitude (1), warmest in south, 16°C (1), coldest in north 13°C (1), hotspots around London and Glasgow (1)

(d) *Level 1* (1–2) basic answer, the further north you go the colder it gets, *Level 2* (3–4) clear answer, temperatures decrease with latitude as the sun's energy has to be spread over a wider area and has a thicker atmosphere to pass through

Population

1 (a) How people are spread out across an area

(b) Unevenly distributed (1), densely populated in e.g. Western Europe (1), India (1), China (1), sparsely populated in e.g. Canada (1), North Africa (1), Brazil (1), Australia (1)

2 *Level 1* (1–2) basic suggestions, no example, e.g. free contraception, *Level 2* (3–4) clear suggestions, named example, e.g. China, limit families to one child each, *Level 3* (5) detailed suggestions, named example, e.g. China, families limited to one child each, permission is required to try for a baby, parents are fined for having a second child, forced abortions have been reported

Settlement

1 (a) 3rd century BC

(b) 10 million

(c) Water supply (1), fuel (1), bridging point (1), soil (1), defence (1)

(d) Focus of roads throughout France and Europe (1), international airports provide global links (1), centre of European rail networks (1)

Agriculture

1 (a) River flowing through a field (1), scattered trees(1) river is full of algae (1),

(b) Sprayed from tractors or aeroplanes (1) to provide nutrients for crops (1)

(c) *Level 1* (1–2) basic descriptive answer, e.g. nitrates harm wildlife, *Level 2* (3–4) clear explanatory answer, e.g. nitrates collect in rivers and lakes, algae grows, taking up oxygen from the water, *Level 3* (5–6) detailed explanatory answer, e.g. farmers overuse nitrates, washed into rivers and lakes by surface run-off and throughflow, encourage algae to grow, decreases oxygen, fish die, nitrates in drinking water are health hazard for people

Industry

1 (a) Industry based on technology rather than heavy raw materials

(b) Not tied to one location (1), most important location factors are transport (1) and labour (1)

(c) South (1), M4 corridor (1), North-east (1), central Scotland (1)

(d) Concentration of skilled and educated workforce (1), motorways give good access (1), close to major cities (1), government grants to attract industry (1), lower wages (1)

Tourism

1 (a) East Africa

(b) Nairobi

(c) Mountainous in the west (1), flat in the east (1), rift valley runs through the centre (1)

(d) Employment (1), money (1), improved services (1), improved standards of living (1)

(e) e.g. fishermen banned from fishing in national maritime parks (1), beaches only accessible to tourists (1), locals no longer allowed to collect seafood (1), villagers' land taken to build hotels (1), coral damaged by careless tourists (1), Masaai forced out of game reserves (1), soil erosion from minibuses (1)

Resources

1 A = Oil refinery
B = Pipeline
C = Oil field
D = Gas field
E = Oil rig

2 (a) Formed from remains of organisms which lived hundreds of millions of years ago

(b) Advantages = easy to transport by pipeline and tanker (1), produce only half the amount of greenhouse gases compared to coal (1), disadvantages = limited reserves (1), damage caused by oil spills (1)

Development

1 (a) Transfer of money (1) or resources (1) from one country to another

(b) North America (1), Western Europe (1), Japan (1), Australia (1)

(c) South America (1), Africa (1), Asia (1), Nicaragua (1), Guyana (1), Surinam (1), Gabon (1), Namibia (1), Zambia (1), Jordan (1), Philippines (1)

(d) Advantages = saves lives (1), improves standards of living (1), opens markets (1), provides jobs (1), disadvantages = increases debt (1), undercuts local producers (1), involves inappropriate technology (1), corruption (1), damages environment (1)

Ecosystems

1 A = Humus
B = Sandy layer
C = Waterlogged layer
D = Iron hard pan
E = Bedrock

2 (a) Wide band between 50°N and the Arctic Circle (1), Northern Europe (1), Siberia (1), USA (1), Canada (1)

(b) Long winters (1), average temperature −28°C (1), short summers (1), average temperature 15°C (1), low precipitation (1) average 25 mm per month (1)

Global environmental concerns

1 (a) Antarctica

(b) Absorbs and filters ultra-violet (UV) radiation from the sun

(c) Release of chloroflourocarbons (CFCs) into the atmosphere (1) from aerosols (1), fridges (1), foam packaging (1)

(d) *Level 1* (1–2) basic ideas, e.g. increase in skin cancer, *Level 2* (3–4) clear ideas, e.g. increase in skin cancer in countries close to the hole in the ozone layer such as Australia, damage to marine ecosystems such as coral as UV **radiation can penetrate through water**